Achilles and Hector

Achilles and Hector
The Homeric Hero

Seth Benardete

Edited by Ronna Burger
Preface by Michael Davis

St. Augustine's Press
South Bend, Indiana
2005

1 2 3 4 5 6   10 09 08 07 06 05

Library of Congress Cataloging in Publication Data
Benardete, Seth.
    Achilles and Hector : the Homeric hero / Seth Benardete ; edited by Ronna Burger ; preface by Michael Davis.
      p. cm.
    "The original publication of this work was from the *St. John's Review*, in two parts, in 1985" – T.p. verso.
    ISBN 1-58731-000-7 (alk. paper) – ISBN 1-58731-001-5 (pbk. : alk. paper)
    1. Homer. Iliad. 2. Homer – Characters – Heroes. 3. Achilles (Greek mythology) in literature. 4. Hector (Legendary character) in literature. 5. Epic poetry, Greek – History and criticism. 6. Trojan War – Literature and the war. 7. Greek language – Epithets. 8. Heroes in literature. 9. Homer – Language. I. Burger, Ronna, 1947– II. Title.
  PA4037.B415 2004
  883'.01 – dc22   2004011861

∞ The paper used in this publication meets the minimum requirements of the American National Standard for Information Sciences – Permanence of Paper for Printed Materials, ANSI Z39.48-1984.

St. Augustine's Press
www.staugustine.net

CONTENTS

Preface

Perhaps it was his appreciation of the tragedy and comedy of life that gave Seth Benardete such delight in titles at once deeply serious and brilliantly playful. Late in his life Benardete published *The Bow and the Lyre: A Platonic Reading of the Odyssey*[1] – the culmination of over forty years of reflection on Homer's *Odyssey*. In the Preface, surveying his own experience, Benardete remarks that Plato so consistently provided him with access to Greek poetry that he was forced to wonder whether Plato had not so much transformed poetic knowledge into philosophy as learned what he knew from the poets. If so, it would be necessary to rethink the "ancient quarrel between philosophy and poetry" that Plato first made thematic. This, no small matter, in the end would require that we rethink as well the relation between thought and action, and with it the very nature of the human soul. The "Platonic wisdom" of the Odyssey is at its heart an account of the intimate connection between the irrational and the rational – the bow and the lyre. The main title of Benardete's first published book on Homer thus stands to its subtitle as Homer stands to Plato and as poetry stands to philosophy. The question of the principle that at once unites and divides them lurks within the colon.[2]

At the same time, the main title itself divides in two. Homer's poem is about Odysseus, a hero adept at both action (the bow) and poetic reflection (the lyre). Homer himself suggests that the two might be one when he describes Odysseus stringing his "singing bow" as though it were a lyre.[3] For us, naturally, a bow is also an instrument for playing a stringed instrument. Homer, of course, wrote another poem, the *Iliad*, ordinarily understood to stand to the *Odyssey* as war stands to peace. So, Homer divides action from thought in his two poems and then divides action and thought in the poem understood to be about thought – Odysseus serves as both actor and narrator of his own actions in the *Odyssey*.

Benardete's title goes at least one duplicitous step further in a pun. The characteristic of poetry is that it speaks "lies like the truth" (the various monsters of the *Odyssey* all occur in the books that Odysseus narrates), whether

1. Lanham, Maryland: Rowman and Littlefield Publishers, 1997.
2. For another title in which the colon is central consider *Socrates' Second Sailing: On Plato's Republic*.
3. *The Bow and the Lyre*, 154.

by impersonation (making one look like two) or by speaking non-literally (making two look like one).[4] The pun, lyre/liar, suggests that within poetry there is still another concealed dyad – with an active part and a reflective part. Homer repeatedly separates the two as a means to show us that and why they can be neither simply separated nor simply put together. This problematic togetherness – the dyad of beast and god in man – is the theme of the *Odyssey*. On the one hand, "the *Odyssey* begins with a man in whom anonymity is coupled with knowledge: he wandered very far, saw the cities of many men, and came to know their mind."[5] After Odysseus names himself "no one" (*outis*) to the cyclops, Homer follows up his lie with a pun on another word for no one, *mêtis* – which with a change of accent can mean mind. The anonymity of mind seems to be the necessary condition for genuine objectivity. It characterizes the Odysseus who traps himself in the Cyclops' cave out of pure curiosity, who in his desire to be in the know about where he is belongs nowhere in particular. On the other hand, there is the Odysseus who is named by his grandfather from the verb *odussomai* – meaning either to be angry at or to be the object of anger.[6] This is the Odysseus who longs for home and whose mind is firmly fixed on avenging the suitors' insult to his name. This Odysseus forces his men to leave the land of the Lotus eaters so that they will not to lose their memories and refuses for himself Calypso's offer of immortality. The problem is to fit the two Odysseuses – the self-negating thinker and the self-affirming actor – together, or rather to see how the two are always already necessarily one. In their problematic unity, Homer finds the nature of man.

This "Platonic" complexity of the peace poem suggests that we may need to rethink as well our view of the war poem, the poem thought to be about action. Perhaps the *Iliad* and the *Odyssey* as a pair are a one that only look like a two. As a guide for Homeric inquiries generally, Seth Benardete is unsurpassed. For the *Iliad* in particular, his *Achilles and Hector: The Homeric Hero* proves indispensable.[7] Like *The Bow and the Lyre*, this, Benardete's only written treatment of the *Iliad* as a whole, bears an intriguing title. It is a book about Achilles and Hector, whose problematic "final identity," comprises *the* Homeric hero.[8] To guide us gradually to the meaning of this identity in the "tragedy of Achilles,"[9] Benardete must prepare the way. With this end in mind, he divides his book into two parts – the first on style, the second on plot.

While the style in question is, in a way, Homer's (Benardete engages in a

4. *The Bow and the Lyre*, xiii.
5. *The Bow and the Lyre*, 3.
6. *The Bow and the Lyre*, 15, 49.
7. See as well Benardete's "Achilles and the *Iliad*" and "The *Aristeia* of Diomedes and the Plot of the *Iliad*" both in *The Argument of the Action: Essays on Greek Poetry and Philosophy* (Chicago: University of Chicago Press, 2000).
8. *Achilles and Hector*, Part II, Chapter VIII.
9. *Achilles and Hector*, Part I, Introduction. See also Part I, Chapter XI and Part II, Introduction and Chapters I, III, V, VI, IX, and XI.

minute analysis of the role of heroic epithets), it refers as well to the style of the Homeric hero, "all that the heroes have most in common."[10] Part I of *Achilles and Hector* means to provide the foundational pillars for our understanding of the Homeric hero. Echoing Aristotle's remarks about the relation between the foreign and the ordinary in poetry,[11] Benardete calls attention to Homer's use of formulae as a way to strike a mean between the "whirlpool of anarchic invention and the rock of listless monotony."[12] Homer "whether by genius or art" finds a way to combine motion and rest in his poetry, for he uses the repetition of formulaic language to organize a story characterized by an otherwise unlimited array of men and actions but then artfully reveals the real truth and underlying instability of this order with the unexpected and unusual use of the formulaic.[13] In calling this "Homer's style and our own method," Benardete indicates that he too needs to stabilize certain terms before demonstrating the structure of their inherent instability. Accordingly, in Part I he develops a series of interrelated pairs.[14] Human being (*anthrôpos*) is understood as what allows us to couple man and woman. Man (*anêr*) is understood first in opposition to woman, and then to human being. Unlike human being, man seems of the same order as god, differing only in scale. Yet this difference gets magnified under the lens of death. Words are associated with human beings, deeds with men, and yet the goal of deeds, immortality, can only be attained in words. These pairs are linked with others – Achaeans, by going into battle in silence, are able to communicate with each other, and hence to act as a unit, while the Trojans, with their exuberant battle cries are not. "Well-greaved" Achaeans, able to shed their armor, are therefore more than their armor – their natures are not exhausted by what they show themselves to be in battle. This is not true of the "high-spirited" Trojans, whose nature in war is the same as their nature simply. Benardete thus shows us how Homer sings of arms and of man, of convention and nature. These terms, and the others Benardete develops in the course of Part I, are his equivalent of the Homeric epithets and are a prelude to his treatment of "the tragedy of Achilles" in Part II.

The plot of the *Iliad* moves through three stages. The first marks the gradual erosion of the original reason for the war – the theft of Helen; it begins with the quarrel of Achilles and Agamemnon and ends with the monomachia

10. *Achilles and Hector*, Part I, Introduction.
11. *Aristotle – On Poetics*, translated by Seth Benardete and Michael Davis (South Bend, Indiana: St. Augustine's Press, 2002), chapter 21. Although he does not cite *On Poetics* in *Achilles and Hector*, Benardete seems to agree with Aristotle in his understanding of the limits placed on poetry and on language generally as well as with Aristotle's habit of sometimes treating the *Iliad* as a tragedy (see especially chapters 8, 15, 23, and 24).
12. *Achilles and Hector*, Part I, Introduction.
13. *Achilles and Hector*, Part I, Introduction.
14. *Achilles and Hector*, Part I, Introduction.

of Menelaus and Paris in Book 3. Glory, the desire to be best and preeminent among men, replaces Helen as the motive for fighting in the second stage, which is marked by the monomachia between Ajax and Hector in Book 7. The final stage of the poem is an unstable synthesis of the first two; here avenging Patroclus is the motive for fighting and it leads to the death of Hector at the hands of Achilles. This movement first establishes the ground for heroic long-ing and then makes manifest its tragedy. Coming from different directions – Achilles having declared his independence from the political and Hector as "a civil Achilles"[15] – the two finally merge by way of Patroclus. The guilt of Achilles for the death of Patroclus – his half-aware willingness to send his friend to death in order to extirpate himself from his self-imposed dilemma – points the way to Benardete's powerful statement of the tragedy implicit in the life of the Homeric hero, a hero whose longing for the immortal is without realizing it a wish to be embalmed – to become like his armor, a thing, or per-haps to come to be identical to his epithet. Not unlike the *Odyssey*, then, the *Iliad* has as its underlying concern the meaning behind, and the paradox with-in, the human longing for immortality.

Written over forty years before *The Bow and the Lyre, Achilles and Hector* might well be thought to be a young man's book. Benardete recounts its origin as having a certain audacity. In an anecdote reminiscent of both Descartes and Nietzsche, he reports that although he had been thinking about the *Iliad* for some time, he "had all these notes, but nothing made any sense." Having resolved to read the poem through quickly from beginning to end, he finished in three days in a stove heated room in the Pensione Bartoletti in Florence. Then, in a burst of insight he saw that the *Iliad* followed the struc-ture outlined in Diotima's speech in Plato's *Symposium*. Following this thread through the plot of the poem, he was able to finish the whole dissertation in a month.[16]

Thirty years after submitting *Achilles and Hector: the Homeric Hero* to the University of Chicago as a doctoral dissertation, Benardete consented to its publication with a brief note (included in this edition) appended to explain what he took to be two related errors.[17] Each error turns on a neglect of the importance of plot. Benardete claims first to have looked too narrowly in his attempt "to vindicate the epithets" attached to the characters of the *Iliad* – he should have looked instead at "the larger units of action." His second error

---

15. *Achilles and Hector*, Part II, Chapter VIII.
16. The quotation as well as the anecdote as a whole is from Seth Benardete, *Encounters and Reflections: Conversations with Seth Benardete*, edited by Ronna Burger (Chicago: University of Chicago Press, 2002), 67.
17. *Achilles and Hector: The Homeric Hero* was published in two parts in consecu-tive issues of *The St. John's Review*, Vol. 36, Numbers 2 and 3, Spring and Summer 1985.

was to note transformations in the structure of the action of the plot without understanding how the causes of these transformations were internal to the action itself. One might say, the mature Benardete chides the young Benardete for ignoring the unfolding of meaning in time by being at once too narrow and too broad in his vision. Now, while we must, of course, take this attempt at self-criticism seriously, it is nevertheless worth noting that while Benardete takes himself to task because "by reading Homer too poetically [he] did not read him poetically enough," he nevertheless did read Homer poetically. His "errors" are perhaps not so discontinuous with his later manner of interpretation as he leads us to believe. After all, by acknowledging in the Introduction that he "inverted the natural order of understanding, and explained first what a hearer would have come to appreciate last," he has already at the outset acknowledged that *Achilles and Hector* begins in error. And his claim that "it would almost not be too rash to assert that if all [the epithets Homer "develops"] were properly understood, the plot of the Iliad would necessarily follow" sounds suspiciously like what he later comes to call "eidetic analysis."[18] In this case, in indicating the errors of *Achilles and Hector*, Benardete may merely have been reaffirming the path one needs to follow in order to understand where he ended up, a concession to time more Homeric than heroic, and hence more Platonic than tragic.[19]

18. *Achilles and Hector*, Part I, Introduction.
19. Compare *Achilles and Hector*, Part I, Chapters V and VII.

Acknowledgments

Seth Benardete's Ph.D. dissertation, "Achilles and Hector: The Homeric Hero," submitted in 1955 to the Committee on Social Thought at the University of Chicago, was published in two issues of the *St. John's Review*, spring and summer 1985. I would like to thank Jane Benardete for permission to reprint it. Robert Williamson's careful work correcting the *St. John's Review* publication is much appreciated, as is Susan Johnson's generous assistance with proofreading. Many people, I'm sure, will share my gratitude to Bruce Fingerhut for making this work more readily available.

Part I
Style

Introduction

This essay falls into two parts. The first part analyzes the style of the Homeric hero, all that the heroes have most in common; the second formulates the plot of the *Iliad*, the tragedy of Achilles. That such a division is possible and even necessary indicates the peculiar nature of the *Iliad*. It is a long work. It can neither be surveyed in a single glance nor remembered in a single hearing. And yet since it is presented as a whole, it must have a certain style to maintain its unity, and a certain kind of subject that will justify its length. Its subject cannot be merely the story of Achilles, for otherwise a short tragedy would suffice, and many of its episodes would be superfluous. Whatever impression one has of Achilles' character does not obviously depend on the whole of the *Iliad*. Many parts, however excellent in themselves, do not seem to advance our knowledge of Achilles and his wrath. The catalogue of ships, the exploits of Diomedes, the deception of Zeus, all seem to reveal Achilles in no clearer light. Only if its scope were as universal as an ancient commentator suggests it is, would its bulk seem warranted:

> Were anyone to ask, noting the worth and excellence of Achilles, why Homer called his work the *Iliad* and not the *Achilleid*, – as he did the *Odyssey* after Odysseus – we would answer that, in one case, the story concerned a single man, while in the other, even if Achilles excelled the rest, yet they too were excellent; and that Homer wished to show us not only Achilles but also, in a way, all heroes, and what sort of men they were: so unwilling to call it after one man, he used the name of a city, which merely suggested the name of Achilles.[1]

Achilles is a hero in a world of heroes; he is of the same cast as they, though we might call him the first impression which has caught each point more finely than later copies. He holds within himself all the heroic virtues that are given singly to others, but his excellence is still the sum of theirs: we do not need a separate rule to measure his supremacy. Golden he may be, but the others shine as brilliant and work as much havoc. Before we can come into the presence of Achilles, and take his measure, we must first be presented with

---

1. Porphyry. *Quaestiones Homericae.*

the common warrior, who is not just something abstract and mechanical but human, and with whom Achilles has more in common than he knows. They are not just gibbering ghosts and mere trophies: they are the armature on which Achilles is shaped and the backdrop against which his tragedy is played. Homer assumes our ignorance of what the heroes are, and like an historical novelist fills the landscape as he advances his plot (it is no accident that the *Odyssey* is shorter), so that their every aspect belongs to his art, until the substance of Achilles, not merely its shadow, can at last be seen and judged; indeed, had not Homer described all of the heroic world, the tragedians would have been unable to select a part and still remain intelligible.

And yet, even if we discover the relevance of the *Iliad's* parts to one another, many of the details within the parts would still be thought needless. That the Achaeans are "well-greaved" and the Trojans "high-spirited" does not evidently pertain to Achilles or the heroes; but again, even were they found to be pertinent, why should Homer have indulged in their repetition? Surely they cannot strike more than a momentary flash in our imagination? They might have served as ornaments, were they not so common: their constant presence makes them tawdry, the burnt-out sparks of a dead tradition; and even if repeated epithets were not tedious, similar scenes, formulaic lines, and identical heroes cannot but burden our memory without improving our knowledge. To answer these charges and grasp the purpose of repetition, we must first consider, in a general way, the style of the *Iliad*.

The *Iliad*, if it is to maintain its unity, demands repetition, but to avoid strain, it needs as well a relaxed grandeur. It must be rapid, easy and spacious. To write like Tacitus, if one wished, like Livy, to record the entire history of Rome, would be intolerable; and to adopt a Livian manner, were one to devote an essay to Agricola, lessens the height of one's opinions. Regardless of temperament, if Tacitus had abused his style, contrary to the needs of the subject itself, and written an universal history, his failure would have been certain; and even as it is, he employs a "choked" syntax, that departs from Ciceronian usage, mostly in his portrayal of Tiberius, whose mastery of dissemblance imposed a similar effort on Tacitus himself. As a student of Thucydides he attempts only small chapters of history, while Livy (like Herodotus) imitates the range of his subject. A rambling work demands a leisurely style; a constricted view must regulate more exactly the stride of each sentence.

Density seems to favor shortness as openness length. A lyric poem is both short and compact; were it longer, its very brilliance would cloy: even Pindar's fourth Pythian, which contains but three hundred lines, is thought excessive. Aeschylus' trimeters are denser than Sophocles', and as a consequence his plays are shorter: not that a single line conveys more matter, but a greater length would shatter the whole. Vergil and Milton, for example, by employing the diction of lyric poetry, often go against the grain of epic. Each line is so overloaded that its luxury saps the strength of the whole, as if the lavishness of their genius packed the work so tightly that it became stunted. The high road of fancy, no matter how inviting it may appear, is closed to the epic poet, even as the thoroughfare of prose would betray his calling. He must steer a middle course between the whirlpool of anarchic invention and the rock of listless monotony; he must restrain his exuberance in each of the parts as he keeps his eye on the whole but still illumine the whole by the light of each part. He cannot adopt a Livian style, containing no limit within itself, whose only virtue is its flexibility, so that it can be stretched to any length; for in achieving a careless ease, he might abandon all the strictures that should limit its extension. A relaxed style seems to guarantee its own dissipation, but as soon as it is stiffened, it may lose, in turn, the only virtue that justified its apparent poverty. And Homer, whether by genius or by art, hit upon a device, partly traditional and partly his own, that at once retained the *sprezzatura* proper to his work as well as informed it into a whole.

Formulae clearly solve a part of this problem. Their familiarity does away with the need for continual invention; their strangeness raises them above the common speech. They will not clutter the work and obscure the whole, nor will they make it vulgar and weaken the whole. They are stage directions. They dispose economically of all the necessary but unimportant actions: walking, speaking, falling and dying, all of which cannot be omitted, even though they may lack significance. Such a diction has great advantages, but if the formulae are merely the cues and promptings to the action, they cannot belong to the whole, however much they may be a part. If they frame the words and deeds, they do not affect their matter. They have no hold on the vital concern of Homer, Achilles and Hector, nor can they pass as his own coinage. They would seem an irreducible surd and a necessary evil. If they are to be fused with the whole, they must reveal something about the heroes, something that distinguishes them from everyone else and from each other, and thus contributes to the theme of the *Iliad*. These differences must exist not only in the large but in the smallest detail, since as Plutarch remarks, "not in the most glorious actions is there always the truest indication of virtue and vice, but often a small occasion, a word, or a gest expresses a man's character more clearly than great sieges, great armaments, and battles with thousands slain; and just as painters catch a likeness from the fact and its features, by which character is expressed, and neglect almost entirely the rest of the body,"[2] so Homer must not lose sight of the smallest occasion, but he must endow each one with a poetic necessity. And yet the vastness of his plan is a hindrance. To present each hero diversely would render them distinct but alien to one another, excessive detail being more likely to break up the whole than restore its unity. Each

2. *Alexander* I.

particular, in choking the whole, would itself be drowned in the others. Homer then, forced to obtain depth without density, realized that the style, which most suited the whole, also could be worked to unite it. Formulae could be repeated without complicating the style: so epithets, were they suggestive enough, could also recur, and in their very recurrence enrich the whole. Their repetition would force us to attend to them and regard them as something more than baubles; so that, even though they are details by themselves, they acquire in the mass sufficient bulk to influence the whole. If, however, they changed their meaning on each occasion, the sum of their ambiguities would disperse their common significance and confound the simplicity of his style; but if they were fixed in meaning, they would not support the otherwise sub-tle portrait of Achilles: they would be thought the burden of a tradition Homer could not shake off. Confronted with these two dangers, infinite variety and idle repetition, Homer struck a balance: he set aside a certain number of occurrences of each epithet as a neutral base, by which the rest are nourished as they reveal its various aspects. Some are unaffected by the passage in which they stand (preserving the clarity); others are closely linked with their context (increasing the depth). The two kinds, though diverse, do not contradict but supplement one another: neither can be sacrificed. The first shows us how essential the epithets are to a hero, the conventions he must observe before he strikes out on his own; the second illustrates these common attributes in action and what they imply: how, when raised to the highest degree, they entail Achilles' tragedy. Neutral epithets indicate how impossible it is for the heroes to cast off their general character, even if these virtues are not required at the moment; pregnant epithets, on the other hand, show themselves in action and explain why the heroes must carry them wherever they go.[3]

One cannot build a palace out of bricks, nor an epic out of separate words; the longer the phrase that can be heard as a unit, the less each part will be swallowed up in the whole. Although precision cannot be discarded, it must have a measure far different from a sonnet's. There must be boldness and dash in epic precision: the broad strokes of painting rather than the sharp exactness of the engraver's art. Every brush mark, regarded closely, neither shares in the whole, nor affects its design. All it presents is a blur of color, seemingly indif-ferent to any larger purpose; but as soon as we view the *Iliad* at its proper dis-tance, what seemed at first superfluous, assumes the appearance of necessity. Yet how could Homer ensure that we would observe the correct distance, and not destroy his work by a too minute inspection? Happily there was already at hand a measure in recitation. Recitation guaranteed that no one would count

---

3.   It was Milman Parry's error not to realize that the inapplicability of an epithet in some instances did not preclude its relevance in others, and that both kinds were necessary.

the threads in the fabric, but it still allowed every thread to count. It separated primary from secondary effects, which, though distinguishable to a reader's eye, the ear as readily keeps apart as unites. One recital may have sufficed to present the whole, another to explicate the parts, a third or a fourth would be needed to make intelligible the formulae: so we in this essay have inverted the natural order of understanding, and explained first what a hearer would come to appreciate last. The first part cannot stand by itself; it must be reinforced by the overall design; but neither is that completely independent, and in one section (Part II, vii) we have tried to bring them together. Within the framework of the epithets Homer "develops" his heroes, and it would almost not be too rash to assert that, if all of them were properly understood, the plot of the *Iliad* would necessarily follow.

Homer did not invent his formulaic diction: if he had, a certain residue of unworked elements would be absent. A swift ship, a black ship, a hollow ship are to him indifferent, metrical convenience alone dictating their use; and though he was not always careless of things, it was not until the lyric poets that they were made equal in rank to persons. He nevertheless transformed the tradition, for, as we suggested, only a poet extremely conscious of the whole would have employed so much repetition, to which no other folk-epic can offer a parallel.[4] He saw that the tradition could be exploited so as to turn its supposed defect into its greatest virtue. It gave him the means to combine the many and the one; display a massiveness that did not sacrifice delicacy; and thus achieve a balance between the generic and the individual, uniformity and diversity, that has always been the despair of the inferior poets. A tragedian, it is true, does not face this problem: he can always join, without intermediaries, the part with the whole, since his hero occupies all of the canvas, and every image and figure works directly for a single end. The details and the design are inseparable, and either immediately leads to the other. To show how successfully it can be managed, and yet how unlike to Homer, has prompted us to trace the imagery of Shakespeare's *Coriolanus* at the end of the second Introduction. There are other reasons as well that made us examine this play; but it suffices to refer to it now as an example of the differences inherent in a short and a long work.

Although Vergil more inclined than Homer did to busy himself with detail (at the expense of the whole), yet he borrowed from him some of his technique; and before we exemplify the previous remarks with an Homeric instance, it is instructive to consider a much simpler one in Vergil. Aeneas is often called "Pius."[5] Sometimes it is obviously apt, and even if it were not his

4.   C. M. Bowra, *Heroic Poetry,* pp. 233ff.
5.   Latin *pius* has a range of meaning which is wider than "pious" or "reverent," e.g., "dutiful," "obedient," "upright."

peculiar badge, we would understand at once why Vergil employed it. When he has buried his nurse Caieta,

> *at pius exsequiis Aeneas rite solutis. . .* [6]
> (But *pius* Aeneas, when the funeral rites were duly paid . . .)

no one would object to its insertion, since the rites Aeneas performs clearly demand it; nor even when Aeneas calls himself *"Pius,"* for not only is it right to assert his piety before Venus, but the rest of the line explains the epithet,

> *sum pius Aeneas, raptor qui ex hoste penatis*
> *classe veho mecum . . .* [7]
> (I am *Pius* Aeneas, who carry with me in my fleet my household
> gods, snatched from the foe . . .)

whoever would think first of his household gods, in a moment of great danger, eminently deserves such a title. Sometimes, however, it is not at all obvious why Aeneas should be thus distinguished, and yet it should not be called even then an idle or an ornamental epithet. When Aeneas attacks Mezentius, *tum pius Aeneas hastam iacit* (then pius Aeneas casts a spear)[8], not so much because Mezentius is *"comtemptor deum"* ("scorner of the gods") is Aeneas glorified,[9] as because Aeneas must be shown to be pious even in war. That is what he is no matter what he does. The action does not explain the epithet, but the epithet is nevertheless its complement. It is the basis on which Aeneas' prowess rests, and as without it, he would not be what he is, Vergil employs it in its most extreme consequences, where it is not visibly effective and yet not wholly powerless. The particular action and the generic epithet are indissolubly linked, not in some mechanical way, so that Aeneas will not only be *pius* when he pays homage to the gods, but also when he fights, and especially when he fights an irreligious man.

As Homer works on an even larger scale than Vergil, his technique differs radically. He must give more examples of the neutral as well as of the pregnant epithet. He must impress upon the audience not only how minimal the virtue in an epithet may be, but also how much greatness it can, when evoked, suggest. An epithet that shows an extraordinary range is *amymôn*, which sometimes means a routine efficiency and sometimes a moral blamelessness. When Homer says,

> For [Achilles] was by far the best, and the horses also, who carried the blameless (*amymôn*) son of Peleus,[10]

6.   *Aeneid* 7. 5.
7.   *Ibid.* 1. 378–379.
8.   *Ibid.* 10. 783.
9.   *Ibid.* 8. 7; cf. 10. 812 and Servius *ad loc.,* 826.
10.   *Iliad* 2. 769–770.

he sets its meaning very high: as best of the Achaeans, Achilles is blameless, even as the mortal horse he yokes in with his immortal horses deserves the same recognition;[11] but when in the *Odyssey* he calls Aegisthus blameless,[12] he sets its meaning at the very lowest mark. Great virtue can exist with great baseness: Aegisthus was of good family, bold (Nestor is partisan when he calls him a coward),[13] and surely as excellent as Antinous and Eurymachus, the worst of Penelope's suitors, who yet excelled all the others in virtue.[14] Between Achilles and Aegisthus lies the whole range of virtue, whose indifference to morality the *Odyssey* makes clear.

When, however, Athena looks for "godlike Pandarus," in order that she might urge him to renew the war, and finds him, the "strong and blameless son of Lycaon," the irony in his perfection is obvious: he is an excellent bowman but a fool.[15] Homer takes care that such a twist may not be lost on the hearer, for he repeats the same lines later, when Aeneas reproaches Pandarus for not employing his skill, and he insists that he did all he could in vain: he should have left his bow at home.[16] It is its repetition within a changed setting that marks the epithet as a variant on its common significance. As Pandarus is a blameless bowman but blameworthy for his attempt on Menelaus' life, so he is innocent of Aeneas' accusation, but he ought never to have brought his bow. And again, the epithet seems to be charged with a different feeling when the dying Patroclus predicts that "blameless Achilles" shall kill Hector,[17] as if he were forgiving Achilles for sending him to his death – Patroclus whom Homer himself calls blameless after his death.[18] To restrict the epithets to mere efficiency in these scenes, or to deny that the audience would respond to them, deprives the *Iliad* of half its effect and turns it into a scrapheap.

"Ajax in his blameless heart knew – and shuddered before – the works of the gods, that Zeus it was who completely thwarted the battle and wished the Trojans victory."[19] If Ajax now retreats, he cannot be blamed, for conscious of his courage, he is not ashamed to yield when Zeus favors the Trojans. *Kata thymon amymona* is unique in the *Iliad,* and hence is proof against all charges of metrical convenience; and since it agrees so well with the passage, it cannot be dismissed as accidental. Poulydamas is often called blameless,[20] and though it seems at first ornamental, as we watch him in action, the epithet fills

11. *Ibid.* 16. 152.
12. *Odyssey* 1. 29.
13. *Ibid.* 3. 310.
14. *Ibid.* 4. 628–629; cf. 17. 381; 22. 241–245.
15. *Iliad* 4. 89, 104.
16. *Ibid.* 5. 169–216.
17. *Ibid.* 16. 854.
18. *Ibid.* 17. 10, 379; cf. 11. 654.
19. *Ibid.* 16. 119–121; *Odyssey* 10. 46–53.
20. *Ibid.* 11. 57; 12. 88; 13. 790; 14. 469.

out and is explained. He first obtains it in a list of heroes, where, though it plays no role, it prepares us for his blameless advice thereafter; which Hector at first accepts but later, to his sorrow, ignores.[21] Homer, in fact, goes out of his way to confer upon him this epithet; for, when *amymôn* no longer fits the metre, he substitutes another word (perhaps his own invention) to express the same thing: "The other Trojans obeyed the plan of blameless (*amômêtoio*) Poulydamas, but Asius was unwilling."[22]

Examples could be multiplied, but these suffice to indicate Homer's style and our own method. An epithet must not be considered a useless relic: each contains a real part of the *Iliad*. Each is worked so expertly as to cement the great with the small, and yet never lose its own identity. Together they give an easy flow to the whole, even as they add a solid intricacy. No other poet has reconciled so well the subtle and the massive: we would have to look to Plato for an equal success, who joined repetition with variety and the universal with the particular to an even greater degree; and though in this he surpasses Homer, he himself acknowledges no worthier rival.

---

21. *Ibid.* 18. 249–252; 22. 99–103.
22. *Ibid.* 12. 108–110.

Chapter I
Men and Heroes

When Hector's challenge to a duel found no takers among the Achaeans, "as ashamed to ignore as afraid to accept it," Menelaus, after some time, adopting a rebuke invented by Thersites, berates them thus:

> ô moi apeilêtêres, Achaiides, ouket'Achaioi[1]
> (Ah me, you boasters, you women, no longer men, of Achaea).

Warriors ought to believe that to be a woman is the worst calamity; and yet Homer seems to mock their belief, in making Menelaus, who warred to recover the most beautiful of women, and Thersites, the ugliest person who came to Troy, the spokesmen for manliness. However this may be, both the Achaeans and Trojans not only insist on being men as opposed to women, but also on being *andres* as distinct from *anthrôpoi*.

Anthrôpoi are men and women collectively, and men or women indifferently: and whatever may be the virtues of an *anthrôpos* it cannot be martial courage, which is the specific virtue of men. Nestor urges the Acheans to stand their ground:

> My friends, be men (*aneres*), and put shame of other humans (*anthrôpoi*) in your hearts, and remember, each of you, your children and wives, your possessions and parents.[2]

The Achaeans themselves must be *andres*,[3] or "he-men"; others, their own children, parents and wives, are *anthrôpoi. Anthrôpoi,* or "human beings," are others, either those who lived before – *proterio anthrôpoi*;[4] – or those yet to come – *opsigonoi anthrôpoi*;[5] and if the heroes employ it of the living, they are careful not to include themselves. Agamemnon swears that he has not touched Briseis, and even if he had, he would not have sinned very much, doing

1. *Iliad* 7. 96; cf. 2. 235; 7. 235–236; 11. 389; 23. 409.
2. *Ibid.* 15. 661–663.
3. *Anêr* is a singular form; plural forms are *andres, aneres*.
4. *Ibid.* 5. 637; 23. 332, 790; cf. 1. 250; 6. 202; 20. 217, 220, 233; 24. 535.
5. *Ibid.* 3. 287, 353. 460; 6. 358; 7. 87.

hê themis anthrôpôn pelei andrôn êde gynaikôn[6]
(as goes the way of human beings, both men and women).

But Odysseus, though he repeats the rest of Agamemnon's speech almost exactly, changes this one line, when he addresses Achilles:

hê themis estin, anax, ê t' andrôn ê te gynaikôn[7]
(as is the way, my Lord, either of men or of women).

Odysseus is aware that Achilles will find that oath more difficult to believe than Agamemnon's other promises; and so by a personal appeal, "my Lord," he hopes to remind Achilles that he too is subject to the same passion, and thus Agamemnon's show of abstinence is all the more to be admired; but lest he risk Achilles' anger, were he to number him among human beings, Odysseus omits *anthrôpoi* and distinguishes (by "either/or") between men and women, whom Agamemnon had classed together. That Achilles, in spite of Odysseus' precaution, does not credit the oath, and that he would have taken offense had Odysseus called him human, his reply indicates; for he places Menelaus and Agamemnon among *meropes anthrôpoi* (literally, humans endowed with speech) though it can only there mean husbands, and calls himself *anêr agathos kai echephrôn* ("a good and sensible man").[8]

Others are *anthrôpoi,* but never is another an *anthrôpos.* If you wish to be an individual, you must be either *anêr* or *gynê,* "man" or "woman"; but if you belong to a crowd, indistinguishable from your neighbor, you are both catalogued together under "human beings."[9] The singular *anthrôpos* occurs but thrice in the *Iliad,* twice in a general sense and perhaps once of an individual, but in all three cases Homer speaks in his own name, and two of them occur in similes.[10] And not only do humans in the heroic view lack all uniqueness and belong more to the past or the future than to the present, but even Odysseus seems to young Antilochus, as a member of a prior generation, more *anthrôpos* than *anêr.*[11] Old age is as absolute as death, which deprives Hector and Patroclus of their "manhood and youthful prime" *(androtêta kai hêbên),*[12] of an heroic manhood that lasts but an instant. Odysseus is consigned to the world of *anthrôpoi* and Hector to Hades.

6.   *Ibid.* 9. 134; cf. BT Scholiast.
7.   *Ibid.* 9. 276.
8.   *Ibid.* 9. 335–337, 340–341. Cf. Hesiod, *Theogony* 416–436; Tyrtaeus fr. 9, 13–14; Aristophanes, *Knights* 1276–1277, 1304; *Thucydides* viii. 73. 3, 92; Xenophon *Hiero* vii. 3.
9.   *Ibid.* 3. 402; 9. 134, 328, 340, 592; 10. 213; 15. 662; 16. 621; 18. 288, 342; 20. 204, 357; 24. 202.
10. *Ibid.* 16. 263, 315; 17. 572.
11. *Ibid.* 23. 787–791.
12. *Ibid.* 16. 857; 22. 363; Cf. 24. 6. The v.1. *ha(a)drotêta* is a corruption of *androtêta* (Cf. Chantraine, *Grammaire Homérique,* I, 110) and is not to be confounded with *adrosynê* (Hesiod, *Works and Days* 473).

Achilles in the ninth book is found "pleasing his heart with the clear-toned lyre and singing the famous deeds of men" (*klea andrôn*)[13]; whereas Aeneas, before declaiming his genealogy to Achilles, remarks that "we know each other's lineage and have heard the famous words of mortal human beings" *(proklyta epea thnêtôn anthrôpôn)*.[14] Deeds are done by *andres,* words are spoken by *anthrôpoi;* and if human beings do anything, it is only the tillage of the fields.[15] The hero's contempt for speeches is but part of his contempt for *anthrôpoi,*[16] and yet they depend on them for the immortality of their own fame.[17] *Anthrôpoi* are the descendants of *andres,* the shadows, as it were, that the heroes cast into the future, where these poor copies of themselves live on; and as the adulation they will give would seem to justify their own existence, it is proper that these later generations, extolling the heroes beyond their worth, should look on them as demigods: so the word *hêmitheoi,* "demigods," occurs but once, in a passage on the future destruction of the Achaeans' wall, and not accidentally it is coupled there with *andres (hêmitheôn genos andrôn).*[18]

Under one condition are the heroes willing to regard themselves as *anthrôpoi:* if they refer at the same time to the gods. Achilles makes the two heralds, Talthybius and Eurybates, witnesses to his oath:

> *Pros te theôn makarôn pros te thnêtôn anthrôpôn*[19]
> (before the blessed gods and mortal men).

The gods are blessed and immortal, while *anthrôpoi* are mortal, and it is only their weakness, when confronted with the splendid power of the gods, that makes the heroes resign themselves to being human. "Shall there be evil war and dread strife," ask the Achaeans and Trojans, "or does Zeus bind us in

13. *Ibid.* 9. 189; cf. 524–527.
14. *Ibid.* 20. 203–204.
15. Cf. *Iliad* 16. 392; 17. 549–550; 19. 131; but cf. Hesiod, *Theogony* 100.
16. Cf. *Iliad* 15. 741; 16. 620–630; 20. 356–368, 248–257.
17. *Iliad* 6. 357–358; 7. 78–91; cf. *Odyssey* 8. 579–580.
18. *Ibid.* 12. 23; cf. W. Schadewaldt, *Iliasstudien,* p. 118, n. 1. The heroes seem in strength more than twice an ordinary man, for they perform deeds which hardly two mortals "such as they now are" could do (*Iliad* 5. 303–304; 12. 447–449; 20. 286–287; cf. 12. 381–383); and at the same time they possess half the strength of the gods, for, though unwilling to resist alone a god-inspired enemy, they think themselves equal if another joins them (13. 55–58, 235–238; 17. 102–104). It would seem that, while the heroes are half-gods, mortals are at most a quarter; and hence the greater frequency of *duo* ("two") with the dual in the *Iliad* than in the *Odyssey* well accords with its theme, as if two sons or two warriors together (taken as a unity) reacquire a divine status (e.g., the two Ajax or the two Atreidae; cf. 2. 679, 822; 4. 393–395; 5. 10, 572). Cf. J. Conda, *Reflections on the Numerals "One" and "Two" in Ancient I-E languages,* pp. 15–20.
19. *Ibid.* 1. 339.

friendship, Zeus who dispenses war to *anthrôpoi?*"[20] Whenever the heroes feel the oppressive weight of their mortality, they become, in their own opinion, like other men, who are always human beings;[21] and the gods also, if they wish to insist on their own superiority, or no longer wish to take care of the heroes, call them in turn *anthrôpoi;* as Athena does, in calming Ares, who has just heard of his son's death:

> For ere now some other, better in his strength and hands than he,
> has been slain or will yet be slain, for it is hard to save the gener-
> ation and offspring of all men (*anthrôpoi*).[22]

If anyone had the right to be called a hero, surely this Ascalaphus, a son of Ares, had; but Athena wishes to point out his worthlessness and deprive him of any divine status, so that Ares' regret at his loss might be diminished. For the gods are not concerned with men insofar as they are mortal, but on the condition of their possible divinity.

How far apart the Achaeans and Trojans are from ordinary men, the word "hero"[23] shows; Homer identifies it with *anêr* (the phrase *hêrôs andres* thrice occurs),[24] and it clearly has nothing to do with *anthrôpoi,* for even we can feel how jarring the union *hêrôs anthrôpoi* would have been.[25] But in what consists the heroic distinction? First, in lineage: the heroes are either sons of gods or can easily find, within a few generations, a divine ancestor; and second, in providence: the gods are concerned with their fate. Zeus is a father to them – "father of men *(andrôn)* and gods" – who pities them and saves them from death, while he is not the father but the king of mortal creations – *hos te theoisi kai anthrôpoisi anassei* ("who is lord over gods and men").[26] Zeus acts toward the heroes as Odysseus was said to treat his subjects – "he was gentle as a father"[27] – and he acts toward us as Agamemnon toward his men: distant, haughty, indifferent. As the providence extended over human beings is unbenevolent, Zeus dispenses war to *anthrôpoi,* himself careless of its consequences; but it is a "father Zeus" who, Agamemnon believes, will aid the

---

20. *Ibid.* 4. 82–84; 19. 224.
21. *Ibid.* 1. 339; 3. 279; 4. 84. 320; 6. 123, 180; 9. 460, 500, 507; 18. 107; 19. 94. 131, 224. 260; 21. 566, 569; 23. 788.
22. *Ibid.* 15. 139–141; cf. 4. 45; 5. 442; 24. 49.
23. Greek, *hêrôs* (singular), *hêrôes* (plural).
24. *Ibid.* 5. 746–747; 9. 524–525; 13. 346; cf. Hesiod, *Works and Days* 159.
25. Hesiod, in his five ages of man, never calls the heroes, unlike the other four ages, *anthrôpoi* (*Works and Days* 109, 137, 143, 180).
26. *Iliad* 2. 669; cf. Vergil. *Aeneid* 1. 65 *passim: divum pater atque hominum rex* ("father of gods and king of men").
27. *Odyssey* 2. 47, 234; 5. 12; cf. *Iliad* 8. 40; 22. 184.

Achaeans and defeat the perfidious Trojans; and as father Zeus he later pities Agamemnon and sends an eagle for an omen.[28]

Andres and *theoi* (gods) belong to the same order: they may be built on different scales, but they are commensurate with one another.[29] Achilles is a *theios anêr*:[30] *theios anthrôpos* would be unthinkable. The direct intervention of the gods seems to elevate man to *anêr,* whereas the flux of fortune, in which no caring providence can be seen, degrades him to *anthrôpos.* "Of all the things that breathe and move upon the earth," Odysseus tells Amphinomus, "the earth nurtures nothing weaker than a human being *(akidnoteron anthrôpoio);* for as long as the gods grant him virtue and his limbs are strong, he thinks he will meet with no evil in the future; but whenever the blessed gods assign him sorrows, then he bears them, though struck with grief, with a steadfast heart."[31] When, however, Zeus pities the horses of Achilles, who weep for Patroclus, he regrets that he gave to mortal Peleus horses ageless and immortal, for "of all the things that breathe and move upon the earth, nothing is more pitiful than a he-man *(oïzyrôteron andros).*"[32] Odysseus talks of *anthrôpoi;* Zeus is concerned only with *andres,* those among us whom the gods favor and try to raise above the common lot of mankind. It is not the uncertainty in man's life which seems to Zeus man's sorrow; for the gods can put an end to chance and ensure his success: but even the gods are powerless to change man's fate no matter how many gifts they might lavish on him. Mortality and mortality alone makes for the misery of man. Odysseus, on the other hand, did not find man's burden in mortality (already implied in *anthrôpos)* but in his inability to guarantee, as long as he lives, his happiness. Not his necessary death, in spite of the gods' attention, but his necessary helplessness, because of the gods' wilful despotism, seems to Odysseus the weakness of man.

Although Zeus and Odysseus here state the human and divine opinions about man's nature, they also reflect, in a more general way, the difference between the *Iliad* and the *Odyssey.* Zeus spoke in one, Odysseus in the other. The *Iliad* is an image of a war-torn world, and as such is but a partial view of the world around us. This deficiency the *Odyssey* corrects, for it more accurately depicts the simply human things. Not man protected by the gods (man at war), but man without the gods, is the subject of the *Odyssey.* Odysseus

28. *Iliad* 4. 84; 19. 224; 4. 235; 8. 245; cf. 5. 33; 8. 132, 397; 11. 80, 201; 16. 250; 17. 630.
29. Cf. *Iliad* 19. 95–96.
30. *Iliad* 16. 798; cf. 5. 184–185, 331–332. 839, and how in Pindar *theos* and *anêr* are linked; *Py.* 4. 21–23; 5. 123; 12. 22; *Ne.* 1. 8–9; 3. 23; fr. 224, 225 (Schroeder).
31. *Odyssey* 18. 130–135; cf. *Iliad* 24. 49.
32. *Iliad* 17. 446–447; cf. 20. 21.

indeed is an exception in his own world, and carries with him some of the providence that was so universal in the *Iliad*. Both Achaeans and Trojans obtained divine assistance there: but not one of the gods now favors the suitors; so that, even if providence still works for Odysseus (who must especially be helped against the suitors, *andres hyperphialoi* – "overweening he-men" – that they are),[33] it leaves the rest of the world intact, little affected by the gods' presence: and this is the world of human beings.[34]

Even as the word *anthrôpos* is more frequent in the *Odyssey* than in the *Iliad,* while the word *hêrôs* occurs almost twice as often in the *Iliad,*[35] so Odysseus saw the cities of many men *(anthrôpoi),* and Achilles cast into Hades the lives of many heroes.[36] The *Odyssey* takes place after the Trojan war, when those upon whom the heroes had relied for their fame are living and remember in song the deeds of the past.[37] Phemius among the suitors and Demodocus among the Phaeacians celebrate an almost dead heroic world; and Odysseus also, since he shared in that past but never belonged to it, recounts rather than acts out his own adventures. As Odysseus' deeds are only *mythoi* so he himself is an *anthrôpos*[38] not only as opposed to the gods, which even Achilles might allow to be true of himself, but absolutely so.[39] War is the business of *hêrôs andres,* peace of *anthrôpoi;* and as Odysseus never did quite fit into the *Iliad* and was an obscure figure (his greatest exploit occurred at night),[40] he becomes in the *Odyssey* preeminent, while the former great are mere ghosts in Hades, and depend on Odysseus for their power of speech.

The heroes are survivors in the *Odyssey*; they no longer dominate the stage, they are old-fashioned and out of favor. Menelaus is a hero (and often uses the word),[41] but Telemachus becomes a hero only at his court,[42] where the spell of the past still lingers. Laertes is a hero, or rather "hero-oldman" (*gerôn*

---

33. Cf. *Odyssey* 15. 302–307.
34. We can easily measure the difference between the *Iliad* and *Odyssey* if we remember that, when Odysseus tells Eumaeus about his exploits in war – how he loved not the working of the soil nor the care for his household, but always ships and wars and well-polished lances were dear to him – it is told as part of a lie *(Odyssey* 14. 211–228).
35. *Anthrôpos:* 118 in *Odyssey.* 70 in *Iliad; hêrôs*: 73 in *Iliad,* 40 in *Odyssey;* the same applies to *anêr, phôs, brotos.*
36. *Iliad* 1. 3–4, *Odyssey* 1. 3; cf. *Odyssey* 4. 267–268.
37. Cf. *Odyssey* 1. 347–352; 8. 479–480; *Iliad* 8. 492–493, with *Odyssey* 1. 358–359; 21. 352–353.
38. *Odyssey* 1. 219, 236; 7. 212, 307; 8. 552; 11. 363–366; 22. 414–415.
39. Cf. Seiler, H., *Glotta* xxxii. 3/4, p.233, who notes that the expressed opposition of *anthrôpoi-theoi* is more common in the *Iliad* than in the *Odyssey.*
40. Cf. Ovid, *Metamorphoses* xiii. 9–15.
41. *Odyssey* 4. 268, 312, 423, 617; 15. 117, 121.
42. *Ibid.* 4. 21, 303, 312; 15. 62.

hêrôs),[43] who putters about in his garden. Other old men are heroes: Aegyptius, Halitherses, Echeneus;[44] and Eumaeus calls Odysseus, when disguised as an old man, hero.[45] The word has been preserved in the country and remains on the lips of swineherd. It has become an empty title, without any suggestion of force, nor even as an indication of rank, for Moulius, a servant of Amphinomus, can now lay claim to it.[46]

43. *Ibid.* 1. 189; 2. 99; 19. 144; 22. 185; 24. 134.
44. *Ibid.* 2. 15, 157; 7. 155; 11.342; 24. 451.
45. *Ibid.* 14. 97. It is in line with this that Eumaeus himself obtains the once proud title *orchamos andrôn,* "file-leader of he-men."
46. *Odyssey* 18. 423; cf. Eustathius *ad loc.*

Chapter II
Achaeans and Trojans

To Agamemnon's demand for an equal prize in return, were he to give Chryseis back to her father, Achilles objects: "Most worthy Atreides – most rapacious of all! – how will the magnanimous Achaeans give you a prize?"[1] The phrase *megathymoi Achaioi* would not at first draw us to examine it, though we might doubt its suitability, were it not that, after Agamemnon has used it (in echoing Achilles), it never again occurs in the *Iliad.*[2] Not the Achaeans but the Trojans are *megathymoi.*[3] Why then did Achilles employ it? *Megathymos* bears here two senses: "great-spirited" and "greatly generous." Achilles asks Agamemnon on the one hand, how the Achaeans, generous though they are, could give him a prize, when all the spoils are already divided. And he asks him, on the other, how they, indignant at Agamemnon's greed, could grant him anything more. As Achilles himself is often *megathymos,*[4] he transfers his own epithet to all the Achaeans, in the hope that, as his anger rises against Agamemnon, the Achaens, carried along by his rhetoric, will side with him. "Great-spirited" is, as the BT Scholiast remarks, demagogic. The Achaeans should be as indignant as himself; they too should revile Agamemnon's presumption; but Agamemnon twists Achilles' phrase to his own end:

> ... but if the *megathymoi* Achaeans give [me] a prize. suiting it to
> my heart, so as to be worth as much – [5]

Had not Agamemnon wished to echo Achilles' line, the apodosis would have been expressed (e.g. *essontai megathymoi,* "they will be magnanimous"); but proleptically, as it were, he puts his conclusion in the protasis. Disregarding *megathymoi* as "great-spirited" (which Achilles the more intended), he assumes it means, ignoring Achilles' irony, "greatly generous": The Achaeans will give him adequate recompense because they are magnanimous, and know how to prepare a gift agreeable to the spirit of a king.[6] The *thymos* of

1. *Iliad* 1. 122–123.
2. *Ibid* 1. 135; cf. *Odyssey* 24. 57.
3. *Ibid.* 5. 27, 102; 8. 155; 10. 205; 11. 294. 459; 13. 456, 737; 17. 420; 23. 175, 181.
4. *Ibid.* 17. 214; 18. 226; 19. 75; 20. 498; 21. 153; 23. 168; cf. 9. 184. 496.
5. *Ibid.* 1. 135–136.

Agamemnon will find a sympathetic response in the *megas thymos* of the Achaeans. He will have nothing to fear from so liberal an army.

The Trojans are *megathymoi* not in generosity but in martial temper, for their leaders use it as an exhortation,[7] even as Hector urges them, as *hyperthymoi* ("over-spirited") to fight in his absence, or not to let Achilles frighten them.[8] They are "over-spirited" as well as "high-spirited" in Homer's opinion.[9] Their spirit is not only grand but excessive; their exurberance in war turns easily into pure fury.[10] They are in the opinion of others, though not in Homer's, *hyperphialoi,* "over-proud" and "arrogant,"[11] a vice that Homer attributes to Penelope's suitors,[12] whom he also calls *agênores* "super-men," as it were, or "muscle-bound"; and this the Trojans also are.[13] Magnanimity may be a vice or a virtue. It contains for example, the intransigence as well as the fearlessness of Achilles.[14] It recognizes no obstacles and knows no bounds. It is so high-keyed that the slightest jar untunes it; it has no slack to take up, nor any reserve to expend. It is all action and no recoil. Thus the Trojans are "high-spirited" both when they see the blood of Odysseus, and when they see one son of Dares killed and the other in flight.[15] In one case, they are spurred to charge and cluster round Odysseus, while in the other they are crestfallen. Men who are high-spirited flourish on success but cannot withstand adversity. "Their courage rises and falls with their animal spirits. It is sustained on the field of battle by the excitement of action, by the hope of victory, by the strange influence of sympathy,"[16] whereas those more reserved and less outwardly spirited *(menea pneiontes –* Homerically, "breathing furious courage")[17] might accomplish less in victory, but would not fall off so much in defeat. They would possess a resilience and a steadiness the Trojans lack.

Nestor in the Doloneia asks whether anyone would be willing to spy on the Trojans, but he begins by assuming no one would: "Friends, no man, trusting to his bold and steadfast heart *(thymos tolmêeis),* would go among the

6. Cf. *Iliad* 1. 53, 196.
7. *Iliad* 5. 102.
8. *Ibid.* 6. 111; 20. 366.
9. Ibid. 9. 233; 11. 564; 14. 15; 15. 135; 17. 276.
10. Cf. *Iliad* 13. 621–639.
11. *Iliad* 3. 106; 13. 621; 21. 224, 414, 459.
12. *Odyssey* 1. 134; cf. 20. 291–292; 21. 289.
13. *Iliad* 10. 299; cf. 4. 176; *Odyssey* 1. 106 *passim;* cf. O. Hoffman, *Glotta* xxviii. p. 32.
14. *Iliad.* 9. 496; 20. 498.
15. *Ibid.* 11. 459; 5. 27–29.
16. I borrow these lines from Macaulay's portrait of Monmouth, *History* of *England.* I, 464 (Everyman's ed.).
17. *Iliad* 3. 8; 11. 508; 24. 364; but cf. 2. 536, 541.

high-spirited Trojans."[18] Whoever might have a *thymos tolmêeis* would be not only *thymôdês* ("high-spirited") but *tlêmôn* ("stout-hearted") as well. He would be *megathymos* and *megalêtôr,* "high-spirited" and "great-hearted," combined. The *thymos* would bestow daring, the *êtor* ("heart") endurance:[19] the one would match the high spirit of the Trojans, "deaf as the sea, hasty as fire"; the other would keep him steady and patient. Thus Diomedes who is "high-spirited" and "over-spirited" picks as his companion "much-enduring" and "great-hearted" Odysseus:[20] for as he kills Dolon and other Trojans, so Odysseus calms the horses of Rhesus, lest they be unnerved at the sight of blood and corpses.[21] Were then Odysseus' and Diomedes' virtues united in the same person, he would be the best: so Achilles has a *megalêtora thymon* as often as he is *megathymos.*[22] To be able to suffer quietly and act quickly are complementary virtues that in Achilles seem to coalesce. But the Trojans are not, except twice, *megalêtores:* once Hector, who is himself "great-hearted,"[23] urges the Trojans to be so; and once Achilles is surprised that they are.[24]

The Trojans are not only *megathymoi* but also *hippodamoi,* "tamers of horses": one word refers to their spirit in war, the other to their peaceful occupation. They exhibit, however, two aspects of the same character. Their temper in war reflects the temper of the horses they tame in peace: we must think of cavalry officers rather than of trainers and grooms: as if the quick, restive, and irritable humors they subdue in horses rubbed off on themselves.[25] Pandarus calls to the Trojans: "Arise, high-spirited Trojans, goaders of horses."[26] He exhorts them in their martial qualities, both in the nature they inherited and the skill they acquired: they would engage their whole person. In another passage, the "over-spirited Trojans" keep pressing in on Ajax, who sometimes turns to flee and sometimes checks the ranks of "Trojans tamers of horses."[27] Had Homer not wished to indicate how close these two epithets are in meaning, he could have easily found another word or phrase. At any rate, it is one of the few instances where *hippodamoi* occurs in a bat-tie scene, and the only time Homer uses it while there is fighting.[28]

18. *Ibid.* 10. 204–206.
19. Cf. *Iliad* 19. 164–170.
20. Diomedes; *Iliad* 5. 25, 235, 335; 6. 145; 10. 509; cf. 4. 365; 5. 376, 881; Odysseus; 5. 674 (cf. 670); 10. 232, 248, 498; 11. 403; only once is he *megathymos (Odyssey* 15. 2).
21. *Iliad* 10.476–481. 488–493.
22. *Ibid.* 9. 255. 629, 675; 18. 5; 20. 343; 21. 53.
23. *Ibid.* 22. 98.
24. *Ibid.* 8. 523; 21. 55.
25. Cf. Sophocles *Ajax* 548–549; *Odyssey* 18. 261–264.
26. *Iliad* 5. 102; cf. 4. 509; 12. 440.
27. *Ibid.* 11. 564–568.
28. *Ibid.* 4. 355. 509; 8. 110; 12. 440; 17. 230. 418; all in speeches. Similarly, *karê*

After Menelaus and Paris have finished arming themselves, "they walked into the space between the Achaeans and Trojans, and their glances were fearful: wonder held those who beheld them, Trojans tamers of horses and well-greaved Achaeans."[29] Achaeans and Trojans both lack an epithet, when Homer sees them merely as two groups of men;[30] but as soon as Paris and Menelaus impress them with their look, and Homer turns to describe their feelings, they become distinguishable. The Trojans are tamers of horses as the Achaeans are well-greaved: but the epithets are not of the same order. If you see the Trojans, you cannot tell that they train horses; if you see the Achaeans, you know they are well-greaved. They appear well-armed: they may or may not be brave warriors: but the Trojans, all of them, are high-spirited in war. They show, even in their wonder, all of their spirit – as if their surprise, though momentary, stirred them completely and declared their profession, while the surprise of the Achaeans glanced off their greaves.[31] The Trojans are more readily affected than the Achaeans, who can remove their armor and be different in peace than in war: but the Trojans cannot so easily shake off their temper. Their epithets are general and do not particularly belong to an army. If we saw them in peacetime, they would be still "high-spirited" and "tamers of horses." But the Achaeans' epithets describe only their military aspect and offer no clue to their peaceful appearance. We know at once more about the Trojans than about the Achaeans, who are, as it were, many-sided and *polytropoi* "of many turns":[32] there is no Odysseus among the Trojans. Not their outward show but the Trojans' inner fibre impresses Homer; he sees it immediately. The Achaeans, however, wear long hair, are well-greaved and bronze-clad, and their eyes flash; while the Trojans, though no doubt they too are bronze-clad and shielded, display more of themselves, and have a kind of openness in their nature that the Achaeans lack.[33] The Trojans' epithets tell us what they are, those of the Achaeans only hint at what they are.

We learn about the Achaeans – what kind of men they are – before we ever meet the Trojans, whom we first get to know but briefly at the end of the second book; and yet we may say that our knowledge of them both is almost complete by the tenth: for it is remarkable how seldom their distinctive epithets appear in the later books. Although the most sustained and violent engagements take place in Books 11–17, it is not in these books that the epi-

---

konioôntes Achaioi ("long-haired Achaeans"), which we may say is opposed to *hippodamoi* ("tamers of horse"), rarely occurs in battle scenes (*Iliad*. 3. 79; 8. 341).

29. *Ibid*. 3. 341–343.
30. Cf. *Iliad* 2. 123; 3. 111, 274, 297, 319; 15. 390; 16. 564, 770; 20. 2–3.
31. Cf. *Iliad* 19. 74.
32. Cf. *Odyssey* 1. 1.
33. Even the epithet *tachipôloi*. "with swift horses" (of the Danaans), is more "obvious" than the Trojans' *hippodamoi*.

thets of the Trojans and Achaeans are most frequently found; they abound instead in the early books, of which only the fifth and eighth books include great battles, and cluster round interludes in the war rather than in the war itself. *Euknêmides* ("well-greaved") for example, occurs nineteen times in Books 1–10, but only twelve in Books 11–24; *chalkochitônôn* ("bronze-coated") seventeen times in Books 1–10, eight afterwards; and *karê komoóntes* ("long-haired") twenty-two times in Books 2–9, four later. In the case of the Trojans, whose high and excessive spirit has more of a place in war (and hence *megathymoi* and *hyperthymoi* occur throughout the *Iliad),* only *hippodamoi* suffers a like decline: seventeen times in Books 2-10, seven afterwards. When the epithets have served their purpose – to introduce us to the Achaeans and Trojans – and Homer becomes increasingly concerned with Achilles, they are more sparingly used. Another reason why *hippodamoi* is used less frequently is that Homer assigns to the Trojans many more similes (which both supplement and replace the epithet) after the tenth book than before: they obtain two in the first half (one in Book 3 and one in Book 4, but fourteen from Books 13 to 22. Of joint similes – those shared equally with the Achaeans – there are four before Book 10 and nine after. For the Achaeans the opposite holds true: eighteen similes occur in Books 2–9, nine in Books 11–19. The similes complete Homer's description of the Achaeans and Trojans, and as we start from the Achaean side and slowly move across the lines to the Trojan (the plague of the Achaeans turns into the funeral of Hector), so the number of the Achaeans' similes diminishes, while that of the Trojans' increases. We must start then (like Homer) with the Achaean host, which is first presented in the second book, where almost half of its similes occur.

When the Achaeans first assemble, at Agamemnon's command, they seem like a mass of bees that issue in constant stream from a smooth rock and then fly in grape-like clusters to spring flowers: so the Achaeans at first make the earth groan when they come from their tents, and a hum pervades the host, but then, once seated in serious concentration, they are perfectly quiet.[34] But as soon as Agamemnon has finished his disastrous speech, they seem like long waves of the sea that east and south winds agitate – they are disturbed contradictorily, and as thick-set wheat, the shrill west wind shakes them – they are pliant and disordered; and with shouts and cries, whose din reaches up to heaven, they drag their ships down to the sea.[35] In their desire to return home, they forget all discipline: no longer distinguishable as individuals as they were as bees when gathering (slight though that individuality might have been), they become the riot and chaos of wheatfield and sea. So much have they been stirred up, that even after Odysseus has checked them, they return to the

---

34. *Iliad* 2. 87–100.
35. *Ibid.* 2. 144–154.

assembly as they left it, shouting like the tumultuous ocean which breaks against a shore.[36] Later, when they scatter to their tents, their shout is the crash of waves against a high-jutting rock, that waves never leave;[37] yet they are now more singly resolved than before, for only the east wind (no east, south, and west as before) moves them, and they center round one object – Troy's capture – like waves that always drench one rock.[38]

The individuality of the Achaeans, lost after Agamemnon's speech, is slowly restored in the succeeding similes, when they are marshalled and turned once again into disciplined troops. The glint of their arms is like fire; the stamp of their feet like the swelling crash of geese, cranes, and swans; the number of their host like leaves, flowers, and flies in spring.[39] They regain in these animal identities their former status, although they are not yet distinct until the next simile: as shepherds easily recognize their own flock in a pasture, so the leaders ranked the Achaeans for battle.[40] Then the catalogue is made, which completes their ranking, and they seem like fire spread across the whole plain of the Scamander, and the earth quakes like thunder.[41] The Achaeans are marshalled noiselessly: the necessary clang of their weapons and tramp of their feet alone are heard, as if their high spirits had been purged in the assembly and nothing remained but a quiet resolution.

> *Fortissimus in ipso discrimine exercitus est, qui ante discrimen quietissimus.*[42]
> (That army is bravest in the struggle itself, which before the struggle is more quiet.)

Homer made all of the second book as a contrast to the Trojans, who as noisily prepare for war as they advance with cries against the silent Achaeans.[43] And later when the truce is broken, while the Achaeans, in fear of their commanders, silently move like the continuous roll of waves, and the only sounds are commands, "nor would you say they had speech"; the Trojans shouted, like ewes bleating ceaselessly, "nor was their clamor in concert, for the voices were mixed, as the men had been called from many lands."[44] As the Achaeans are silent, they can obey the orders they hear; but the Trojans would drown in their own clamor any command. The simile of the Achaeans is delib-

---

36. *Ibid.* 2. 209–210.
37. *Ibid.* 2. 394–397.
38. Cf. H. Fraenkel, *Die Homerischen Gleichnisse,* p. 20.
39. *Iliad* 2. 455–473; cf. 469 with 87.
40. *Ibid.* 2. 474–477.
41. *Ibid.* 2. 780–785.
42. Tacitus *Hist.* i. 84.
43. *Iliad.* 2. 810; 3. 1–9; cf. Thucydides ii. 89. 9.
44. *Ibid.* 4. 422–438; cf. 2. 804, 867; Aeschylus *Pers.* 401–407; Polybius xv. 12. 8–9; Plutarch *de aud. poet.*10; Milton *Paradise Lost* i. 549–562.

erately inexact, for the echoing shore, against which the waves break, has no counterpart in themselves. No sooner are they compared to the sea, than they are distinguished from it. They are what is inconceivable in nature, an ordered series of silent waves. The Trojans, however, exactly correspond to their simile: myriads of ewes pent up together in confusion. Of the Trojans' other similes in the midst of battle, four single out the clamor they make, as waves, or winds, or storm:[45] but the noise of the Achaeans, even when they do shout,[46] only warrants a simile if the Trojans join in,[47] and they are compared to water but once in battle: when their spirit, not any outward sign, shows vexation.[48]

It is not difficult to see how the epithets of the Trojans are connected with their disorder, nor how those of the Achaeans indicate their discipline. The high-spiritedness of the Trojans would naturally express itself in cries, and the fine greaves of the Achaeans would indicate a deeper efficiency. The ranks of the Trojans never equal in closeness those of the Achaeans, whose spears and shields form a solid wall, shield and helmet of one resting on helmet and shield of another.[49] Nor do the Achaeans, on the other hand, ever retreat like the Trojans:

paptênen de hekastos hopêi phygoi aipyn olethron[50]
(and each looked about, how he might escape sheer destruction).

The Trojans flee, as they attack, in disorder, and more by *thymos* than by *epistêmê* ("knowledge," "skill") are they warriors.[51] They are, in the later Greek vocabulary, barbarians. Thucydides' Brasidas, in urging his troops to face bravely the Illyrians, could be describing the Trojans who "by the loudness of their clamor are insupportable, and whose vain brandishing of weapons appears menacing, but who are unequal in combat to those who resist them; for, lacking all order, they would not be ashamed, when forced, to desert any position, and a battle, wherein each man is master of himself, would give a fine excuse to all for saving their own skins."[52]

How then are we to explain the silent efficiency of the Achaeans and the

45. *Ibid.* 13. 795–800; 15. 381–384; 16. 364–366; 17. 263–266; cf. 12. 138; 16. 78, 373; 21. 10. Once the Trojans attack without shouting *(abromoi auiachoi)* and only then are they compared to fire (13. 39–41); cf. C. Robert, *Studien zur Ilias,* pp. 124–125; U. Wilamowitz, *Die Ilias und Homer,* p. 252. n. 2.
46. *Ibid.* 11. 50; 18. 149.
47. *Ibid.* 4. 452–456; 14. 393–401; 17. 736–740.
48. *Ibid.* 9. 4–8.
49. *Ibid.* 13. 128–133; 16. 212–217.
50. *Ibid.* 14. 507; 16. 283.
51. Cf. Thucydides i. 49. 3; ii. 11. 8, 87. 4–5,89. 5–8.
52. iv. 126. 5; cf. Herodotus vii. 211. 3. 212. 2; viii. 86. One might say that what distinguishes the Achaeans and Trojans persists in Herodotus as the difference between Greeks and Persians, and in Thucydides, on a much higher level, as the difference between Athenians and Spartans.

noisy disorder of the Trojans? Has Homer given a reason for this difference? Is there one principle whose presence would force the Achaeans into discipline and whose absence would let the Trojans sink into anarchy? *Aidôs,* "shame," seems to distinguish them. There are two kinds of *aidôs:* one we may call a mutual or military shame, the other an individual or civil shame.[53] The first induces respect for those who are your equals; or, if fear also is present, your superiors;[54] the second entails respect for those weaker than yourself. The first is in the domain of *andres,* the second of *anthrôpoi.*[55] Hector shows civil shame when, in speaking to Andromache, he says: "I am terribly ashamed before the Trojans, men and women both, if I cringe like someone ignoble and shun battle."[56] And Hector is killed because he would be ashamed to admit his error (of keeping the Trojans in the field after Achilles' reappearance), ashamed lest someone baser than himself might say, "Hector, trusting to his strength, destroyed his people."[57] As commander of his troops, with no one set above him, Hector must either feel the lash of public opinion, or become as disobedient as Achilles, who at first lacks all respect for Agamemnon and later all respect for Hector's corpse.[58]

When, however, the Achaeans silently advance against the Trojans, they show another kind of shame, "desirous in their hearts to defend one another."[59] Their respect is not for others but for themselves. Neither those stronger nor those weaker than themselves urge them to fight, but each wishes to help the other, knowing that in "concerted virtue" resides their own safety.[60] "Be ashamed before one another," shouts Agamemnon (and later Ajax), "in fierce contentions: when men feel shame, more are saved than killed; but when they flee, neither is fame nor any strength acquired."[61] And even when the Achaeans retreat, they do not scatter like the Trojans, but stay by their tents, held by "shame and fear, for they call to one another continuously."[62] Whatever fear they have before their leaders is tempered by their shame before one another; and as, according to Brasidas, three things make men good soldiers – will, shame and obedience –[63] so the Achaeans show their will in preferring war to peace,[64] their shame in mutual respect,[65] and their

53. Consider how in Thucydides virtue and shame are coupled: i. 37. 2, 84. 3; ii. 51. 5; iv. 19. 3; v. 9. 9, 101.
54. Cf. Sophocles *Ajax* 1075–1080; Plato *Euthyphro* 12a7–12c8, *Amatores* 135a3–5 with *Odyssey* 21. 285–286, 323–329.
55. Cf. Aeschylus *Agamemnon* 937–938.
56. *Iliad* 6. 441–443; cf. 8. 147–156; 12. 310–321; 17. 90–95.
57. *Ibid.* 22. 104–107; cf. Aristotle *MM* 1191a5–13, *EE* 1230a16–26.
58. *Ibid.* 24. 44–45.
59. *Iliad* 3. 9; cf. 2. 362–363.
60. *Ibid.* 13. 237.
61. *Ibid.* 5. 52532 15. 561–564.
62. *Ibid.* 15. 657–658; Cf. 8. 345–346; 17. 357–365.
63. Thucydides v. 9. 9; cf. i. 84. 3.

obedience in the fear of their leaders.[66]

Agamemnon as a good king and Ajax as a brave warrior appeal to military shame, when they incite the Achaeans; but aged Nestor urges them in the name of civil virtue: "Friends, be men *(andres)* and place in your spirit shame of other human beings *(anthrôpoi),* and let each of you remember your children, your wives, possessions, and your parents, whether they still live or now are dead; for the sake of those who are not here I beseech you to stand your ground."[67] Even as Nestor has placed his worst troops in the middle, so that they will be forced, though unwilling, to fight,[68] so there he wishes to regard all the Achaeans as caught between the Trojans in front and their own families behind them; and he hopes by this necessity, of avoiding death at the hands of one and humiliation in the eyes of the other, they will resist. Nestor leaves nothing to personal courage: it is of a piece to rely on necessity and to appeal to civil shame; for to a man who has outlived two generations the bonds of society would seem stronger than those of an army, nor would his own weakness give him any confidence in others' strength. As a very old man he has no peers, and all relations seem to him the relation of the young to the old, so that in making the Achaeans respect their parents, he covertly makes them respect himself. Unable to inspire his men by fear of himself and unwilling to trust to military discipline, Nestor falls back on the rehearsal of his own past prowess and on his soldiers' recollection of those absent.[69]

Military shame never once arouses the Trojans whom the cry "Be men!" always encourages; and once, when Sarpedon tries to rally the Lycians – *aidôs ô Lykioi, pose pheygete; nyn thooi este* ("Shame, you Lycians, whither are you fleeing? Be vigorous now!") – the appeal is to civil shame: for as warriors they are urged to be "vigorous," and shame is only invoked to check their flight.[70]

The Trojans rely more on their leaders than on their troops,[71] for we always read of the "Trojans' *and* Hector's" attacking,[72] as if the single virtue of Hector more than equaled the mass effort of his men.[73] If the Trojans act in concert, it is rather by the example of one man than by any bravery in themselves; and Hector himself resembles Xenophon's Proxenus, who "was able to rule those who were noble and brave, but unable to instill shame or fear into

64. *Iliad* 2. 453–454; II.
65. *Ibid.* 5. 787; 8. 228; 13. 95, 122; 15. 502, 561.
66. *Ibid.* 4. 431; cf. 1. 331; 4. 402: 24. 435.
67. *Ibid.* 15. 661–666; cf. Tacitus *Hist.* iv. 18. 4; *Germania* 7–8.
68. *Iliad.* 4. 297–300; cf. Xenophon *Memoribilia* iii. i. 8; Polybius xv. 16. 14. 1–4.
69. Cf. *Iliad* 4. 303–309.
70. *Iliad* 16. 422–430; cf. BT Scholiast 13. 95; 15. 502.
71. Cf. Tacitus *Germania* 30. 2.
72. *Iliad* 13. 1, 129; 15. 42. 304, 327, 449 *passim.*
73. Cf. *Iliad* 13. 49–54.

his own troops, since he actually was more ashamed before his men than they before him."[74] Aeneas, for example, can rouse Hector and the other captains by an appeal to shame, but it would be unthinkable to employ the same argument before all.[75] Though Nestor's call to the Achaeans does appeal to a kind of civil shame, theirs differs in this from the civil shame of the Trojans, which affects only their greatest warriors.

How little the Trojans as a whole are affected by honor or shame, Homer shows us in the Doloneia, where under the secrecy of night the basest motives and the most cowardly actions prevail.[76] Nestor asks an Achaean to volunteer for a night patrol, and as reward he offers great fame under heaven, a black ewe with her lamb from each of the chiefs, and the perpetual right of being present at banquets and feasts.[77] The two last inducements are mere tokens, deliberately intended to be insufficient by themselves; so that the real emphasis might fall on the desire for fame, which would animate only the noblest heroes. When, however, Hector tries to provoke a Trojan to the same exploit, he offers a considerable prize: the best horses and chariot of the Achaeans.[78] The consideration of honor barely obtains mention. Hector does not even think that fame would be an incentive at all, while Nestor makes the material gain so little that fame alone must suffice. The cupidity of Dolon (though his being the only male among five sisters somewhat pardons it) is the extreme example of Trojan shamelessness, while the honorable ambitions of Diomedes, though slightly depreciated by his hesitation, is but the kind of nobility in which all the Achaeans share.

Lessing grasped very well the difference between the Achaeans and Trojans, when he wrote that "what in barbarians springs from fury and hardness, works in the Greeks by principle, in whom heroism, like the spark concealed in flint, sleeps quietly, and as long as no outer force awakens it, robs it of neither its clearness nor its coldness; while barbaric heroism is a clear, devouring flame which always consumes (or at least blackens) every other good quality. If Homer leads the Trojans to battle with wild cries, but the Greeks in resolute silence, the commentators are quite right to observe, that the poet wishes to depict one side as barbarians and the other as a civilized people. I am surprised, however, that another passage, where there is a similar contrast of character, has not been noticed. The enemy leaders have made a truce, and are engaged in the cremation of their dead, which on both sides takes place with much weeping. But Priam forbids the Trojans to weep.[79] 'He

74. Xenophon *Anabasis* ii. vi. 19.
75. *Iliad* 17. 335–341. It is noteworthy how both here and elsewhere (5. 787; 8. 228; 13. 95, 122) the appeal to shame is either said or inspired by a god.
76. Cf. Xenophon *Cyrotaedeia* viii. i. 31.
77. *Iliad* 10. 212–217.
78. *Iliad.* 10. 303–307; cf. BT Scholiast 10. 303; 17. 220.

forbids them to weep,' says Mme. Dacier, 'because he fears they may become soft, and in the morning go into battle with less ardor.' Quite true; but still I ask: Why must Priam alone be afraid of this? Why did not Agamemnon also give the same order? The meaning of the poet goes deeper. He wishes to teach us, that only the civilized Greeks can both weep and be brave, while the barbarous Trojans, in order to be brave, had to stifle all their humanity."[80]

79. *Ibid.* 7. 427 (consider 430); cf. 19. 295–299.

80. Lessing *Laokoon* I.

Chapter III
Achilles and Agamemnon

Achilles and Hector are heroes, one an Achaean, the other a Trojan: but to know them better, so that even away from their camps, we would not mistake them, forces us to find other traits peculiar to themselves. Who then is Achilles? Homer begs a goddess to sing the wrath of "Peleides Achilles."[1] Achilles is the son of Peleus. He is marked off from all other men because of his father: as an only son without brothers, he was entirely Peleus' heir.[2] And were we to ask, Who is Peleus? we would be told: "Aeacides," the son of Aeacus. And if we persisted, and wanted to know who he was, Achilles himself boasts it: "Aeacus was from Zeus."[3] Achilles then is "Zeus-born," "Zeus-nurtured," or "dear to Zeus." In three generations he goes back to Zeus, and beyond him it would be foolish to go. To ask him who he is means to ask him his lineage; and as he can only define himself in terms of his past, were his ancestors unknown, he would be a non-entity.[4] In Achilles' patronymic is summed up part of his own greatness. He is partly the work of generations.

Achilles has so much the springs of all his actions in the past, that Homer can call him "Peleides" without adding "Achilles," though it is Agamemnon, who even more than he depends on his ancestors, that first addresses him so; while Homer calls him "Peleion" for the first time only after Agamemnon has mocked and doubted his divine ancestry.[5]

Achilles, however, is not only the son of Peleus but the grandson of Aeacus; and yet to be called "Aeacides," when he is actually "Peleides," means that he has inherited something that was common to all his ancestors. Achilles is called the son of Aeacus first in the Trojan catalogue: Ennomus and Amphimachus were both killed by Achilles in the guise of "swift-footed Aeacides."[6] Achilles resembles his grandfather in his ability to kill. As a war-

---

1. Whether "Peleides," "Atreides," etc., are patronymica or gentilica has been much disputed; cf. K. Meister, *Die Homerische Kunstsprache*, pp. 149–150; P. Chantraine, *op. cit.*, I, 105–106.
2. *Iliad* 24. 538–540.
3. *Ibid.* 21. 189.
4. Cf. *Iliad* 6. 123 with 145–146; 21. 150 with 153.
5. *Iliad* 1. 146, 188, cf. 178.
6. *Ibid.* 2. 860, 874, but cf. A Scholiast.

rior he is indistinguishable from his forefathers: killing is a family profession.[7] During the embassy, when Achilles is most idle, though ironically most Achilles (for his wrath makes up a great part of him), no one calls him the son of Peleus; rather they point out to him how much he has failed to follow his father's precepts.[8] When, however, he returns to the fighting, his father's name is almost as common as his own; and as he assumes his ancestral name, he takes up his father's spear, which no more could be hurled by another than "Peleides" be said of another;[9] while again, in the last book, where his own name occurs more frequently than anywhere else, his patronymic hardly appears, and he is never called to his face the son of Peleus. Somehow he has outlived it.

As Hector had many brothers, to tell us at first that he is the son of Priam would mean little: so Achilles, who first mentions him, calls him "Hector the man-slayer."[10] Paris, contrariwise, does not even deserve his father's name, for his only distinction lies in his theft: he is most of all the "husband of Helen,"[11] although in his braver moments, which do not last very long, he earns the right, that other heroes have without question, to be called "Priamides."[12]

But when we ask, "Who is Odysseus?" and turn to the first lines of the *Odyssey,* the answer is quite different: "Tell me of the man, Muse, of many wiles who wandered very far." Odysseus is a clever man who wandered very far. He is not made distinct from other men because he is the only son of Laertes, but because he traveled. His genealogy is contained in what he himself did and not in what his father might have been. Laertes' father is known, but his grandfather is unmentioned: tradition indeed gave him two family stems.[13] Homer in the *Iliad* never calls him anything but Odysseus though other heroes address him as if he were like themselves – "Zeus-born Laertiades, very-crafty Odysseus" – but even here his subtlety belongs to himself, while his divine origins (whatever they may have been) belong to his father. Homer in the *Odyssey* calls him "Laertiades," except in a special case,[14] only after he has returned to Ithaca.[15] For twenty years he is merely Odysseus, but he reassumes his lineage as soon as he lays claim to his king-

---

7. Cf. the way each side exhorts their troops in Thucydides, e.g., iv. 92. 7, 95. 3; see also Herodotus vi. 14. 3; viii. 90. 4.
8. *Iliad* 9. 252–259, 438–443.
9. *Ibid.* 19. 387–391; cf. 14. 9–11; 16. 140–144; 21. 174–178; 20. 2.
10. *Ibid.* 1. 242.
11. *Ibid.* 3. 329; 7. 355; 8. 82; 13. 766.
12. *Ibid.* 3. 356; 6. 512.
13. Cf. Pauly's *Realencyclopädie* vxii, 2 col. 1918.
14. *Odyssey* 8. 18.
15. *Ibid.* 16. 455; 17. 361; 18. 348; 20. 286; 22. 191, 339.

dom. His patrimony gives him back his piety.[16] Ovid understood Odysseus when he made him say:

> *Nam genus et proavus et quae non fecimus ipsi, / Vix ea nostra voco.*[17]
>
> (Race and ancestors and what we ourselves have not done, I hard-ly call ours.)

Even the shift from the plural *"fecimus"* to the singular *"voco"* reflects his uniqueness.[18]

Odysseus' adventures are his lineage, making his very name superfluous. He is a traveler, who "saw the cities of many men and knew their mind"; and his name, put almost as an afterthought (without his patronyrnic),[19] cannot make clearer his identity, nor add much lustre to his eminence. He is like Thersites, whose father and country are not given,[20] his deformity and out-spokenness being title enough; so that to have Odysseus, Thersites' closest rival in anonymity, answer his abuses was a master-stroke. Their resemblance is so close that Sophocles' Neoptolemus, when Philoctetes asks about a man "clever and skilled in speaking," thinks he must mean Odysseus, whereas he actually means Thersites.[21] Moreover, Philoctetes, believing it to be a truer lineage, can even call Odysseus the son of Sisyphus; and Odysseus can tell Eumaeus that he is illegitimate.[22]

When Odysseus tells the Cyclops his name – "No-one is my name: my father, my mother, and all my companions call me No-one"[23] – he is speaking more truthfully than when he tells Alcinous that he is the son of Laertes.[24] His anonymity is the result of his guile, for Homer has him pun[25] on the likeness of *outis* and *mêtis*.[26] His wisdom made him no one, and cut all his ties with the past.

16. Cf. *Odyssey* 24. 270. Thucydides refers to himself only once as the son of Orolus; when he is in *command* of Athenian forces (iv. 104. 4); elsewhere, as an histori-an, he is plain Thucydides or Thucydides the Athenian.
17. *Metamorphoses* xiii. 140–141.
18. Cf. *Iliad* 6. 150–151; 20. 213–214.
19. *Odyssey* 1. 21.
20. Cf. BT Scholiast 2. 212.
21. Sophocles *Philoctetes* 440–442.
22. *Ibid.* 417 (cf. *Ajax* 189); *Odyssey* 14. 202–203.
23. *Odyssey* 9. 366–367.
24. *Ibid.* 9. 19; cf. 10. 325–330.
25. The Cyclopes confuse Odysseus' assumed name, *Oûtis*, with *oútis*, "no one" (Od. 9. 366. 408. 410). Odysseus' pun is based on the resemblance of the alternative word for "no one," *métis*, to *mêtis*, "guile," "cunning" (9. 410, 414).
26. *Ibid.* 9. 414, cf. 408.

Although Achilles, if opposed to Odysseus, seems to consist in nothing but his past, yet when opposed to Agamemnon, he becomes more an individual. Indeed, he stands somewhere in between Agamemnon and Odysseus. Agamemnon does not even appear, at first, as himself, but as "Atreides lord of men," while Achilles is "divine" in comparison.[27] Not until he differs from the rest of the Achaeans (who wish to restore Chryseis), though he has been mentioned thrice before, does Homer call him Agamemnon;[28] even so does Achilles call him "Atreides" after he has convened the assembly, but "Agamemnon" when he wishes to single him out for his crime.[29] Agamemnon rises to rebut Achilles, but Homer first clothes him in all possible authority: "Hero Atreides, wide-ruling Agamemnon."[30] This majesty fails to impress Achilles, who begins his reply, however, as if he agreed with him: "Most worthy Atreides," but instead of ending the line, as we later realize he should have, he cruelly inserts: "Most rapacious of all!"[31] The proper end-tag ("lord of men Agamemnon") often occurs, mostly spoken by Nestor, who, old man that he is, knows what loyalty and respect must be shown to a king. When the Achaeans are about to be catalogued, Agamemnon must have full power. He must be not only the "most worthy" because of his lineage, but also the "King of men in his own name."[32] Later, when the fortunes of the Achaeans are lowest, Nestor again bolsters Agamemnon with his titles; and the other kings also, after the embassy to Achilles falls, subscribe in the same way their loyalty.[33] Achilles only much later, when he has sloughed off his rage, addresses him properly.[34]

Not until, however, Achilles swears an oath by Agamemnon's sceptre, does the conflict between them come out in the open: "Yes, by this sceptre, which never again shall grow branches or leaves, since it first left its stump on the mountain, not shall it bloom again, for the bronze blade has stripped it of its leaves and its bark: and now in turn the sons of the Achaeans, the wielders of justice, carry it, those who protect the laws that come from Zeus. . . ."[35] Then he flings down the sceptre, "studded with golden nails." We learn the true origin of this sceptre much later, just before Agamemnon, doing "what is right,"[36] tries the Achaeans, fearful that Achilles' refusal to fight and his desire to return home have infected the army: "Up stood strong Agamemnon with the

27. *Iliad* 1. 7.
28. *Ibid.* 1. 24.
29. *Ibid.* 1. 59, 90, cf. 94.
30. *Ibid.* 1. 102; cf. 7. 322; 13. 112.
31. *Ibid.* 1. 122.
32. *Ibid.* 2. 434, but note 2. 362.
33. *Ibid.* 9. 96, 163, 677, 697 with which cf. 8. 293.
34. *Ibid.* 19. 146, 199; cf. 23. 49.
35. *Ibid.* 1. 234–239.
36. *Ibid.* 2. 73; cf. B Scholiast (Porphyry); Jacoby, F. *SBPAW* 1932, pp. 586–594.

sceptre, which Hephaestus artfully had made: Hephaestus gave it to Zeus lord Cronion, and Zeus gave it to the Treasurer of Riches (who kills with his brilliance), and lord Hermes gave it to Pelops the goader of horses, and Pelops in turn to Atreus the shepherd of his people; and Atreus when he died left it to wealthy Thyestes, and he in turn left it for Agamemnon to wield – to rule over many islands and all Argos."[37] Lessing has beautifully brought out the reason why the one sceptre receives these two descriptions: "This was the work of Hephaestus; that, an unknown hand hewed on a mountain: this belonged of old to a noble house; that to him whose fist first grasped it: this to a king whose rule extended over many islands and all Argos; that, wielded by a man in the midst of the Greeks, to whom was entrusted, with others, the defense of the laws. Here was the real difference between Agamemnon and Achilles, a difference which Achilles himself, in all his blind rage, could not but admit."[38] The conflict between them is between authority and power, between the gifts of nature and those of an heritage. Agamemnon's authority consists in mere words (in the fame of his ancestry), and were Achilles to yield to them, as if they were deeds, he would be thought weak and cowardly.[39] Briseis is only the pretext for this more serious difference, which must always exist, wherever power and position (*potentia* and *potestas*) do not coincide. The usurper Bolingbroke and King Richard II, for example, as made by Shakespeare, work out in more tragic fashion the dispute between Achilles and Agamemnon: for Richard relies as much on his divine appointment as Agamemnon; and Bolingbroke, like Achilles, trusts more to "blood and bone" than to ancestral right.[40]

Achilles swears by the authority of Agamemnon in terms of his own power. He swears by the sceptre as he swears by the gods: and only Achilles swears.[41] Agamemnon calls upon the gods more cautiously, as witnesses (as those who know);[42] whereas the gods to Achilles are no more than this sceptre, which is but the extension of his own power, losing all its force as soon as he casts it aside. Though "studded with golden nails," he holds it in no esteem. Any branch at all – "a palmer's walking-staff" – would serve him as well. He does not need the past to rally the present. But Agamemnon, who has little confidence in his own strength, must lean upon his sceptre, unlike Hector, Achilles' equal, who leans upon a spear while he speaks.[43] Hector's spear is replaceable, while Agamemnon's sceptre is unique: were it broken,

---

37. *Ibid.* 2. 100–108.
38. *Laokoon* xvi.
39. Cf. 1. 293–294.
40. Cf. *Richard II* 3. 2. 54–62; 3. 3. 39–53, 72–90.
41. *Iliad* 1. 86, 339; 23. 43.
42. *Ibid.* 3. 276–280; 19. 258–260.
43. *Ibid.* 2. 109; 8. 496.

Agamemnon would be doomed to obscurity. He swears neither by sceptre nor by gods, but rather he holds up the sceptre to all the gods.[44] His lineage, embodied in the sceptre, connects him with the gods. He looks to them; Achilles looks to himself.

Odysseus alone knows how to combine, in the sceptre, the rank of Agamemnon and the force of Achilles. He stops the general rout of the Achaeans, which Agamemnon's speech had caused, by making a distinction that Achilles would not, and Agamemnon could not, employ.[45] Taking the ancestral sceptre in his hand, he speaks to the kings thus: "If you disobey Agamemnon he shall oppress you; the wrath of a Zeus-nurtured king is great; his honor comes from Zeus, and counseling Zeus loves him."[46] He uses the sceptre as an emblem of power, threatening the kings, who would be unimpressed by mere lineage, with divine vengeance. Authority lies in power. But against anyone of the rank-and-file, Agamemnon's sceptre turns into a weapon: Odysseus drives them before him with it.[47] He speaks to them quite differently: "Sit down without a murmur, and listen to others, who have more authority: many-headed rule is bad; let there be one head, one king, to whom the son of Cronus gave rule.[48] Power lies in authority. As Zeus is Zeus to the kings, but to the common warrior the son of Cronus,[49] so Agamemnon must appear to the kings as authoritative might, but to the warriors as powerful authority.

44. *Ibid.* 7. 412; cf. Aristotle *Politica* 1285b3–12.
45. Cf. Xenophon *Memorabilia* i. ii. 58; iv. vi. 13–15.
46. *Iliad* 2. 185–197; cf. 1. 174–175; ABT Scholiast 2. 186.
47. *Ibid.* 2. 199, cf. 265–266.
48. *Ibid.* 2. 200–205.
49. Cf. *Iliad* 1. 175; 9. 37, 98, 608.

Chapter IV
Ancestral Virtue

It is important that we do not learn the true nature of the charges that Achilles had made against Agamemnon until the second book; that the lineage of the sceptre is not disclosed until then; and that we are kept in suspense about his accusations against Agamemnon – who neither risked his life in ambush, he said, nor ever entered into the battle[1] – until Achilles is no longer present, and his one defender is Thersites.[2] Only in retrospect is Achilles justified.

Homer throughout the first book keeps underlining the struggle between them. Agamemnon scornfully remarks to Achilles: "If you are, in fact, stronger, a god (I suppose) gave it to you."[3] He sees what Achilles is aiming at, and desperately points out to him that, even though Achilles is stronger, a god gave him his strength, so that he really is no different from himself, to whose ancestor Zeus gave the sceptre. Not only does he deny the superiority of Achilles in birth (the source of Agamemnon's strength is Zeus, who is superior to any other god), but he wishes to prove that the gulf between them is not very great, since neither his own authority nor Achilles' strength is properly their own. It is a last-minute stopgap, and naturally it fails to work. But Agamemnon, confident that he has been persuasive, merely asserts what Achilles refuses to acknowledge: "so that you might know how much more powerful [authoritative] I am."[4] Nestor, when he tries to calm them both, adopts Agamemnon's argument. He calls Achilles "Peleides," hoping to remind him of his ancestry, and then: "If you are stronger, a goddess was your mother; but he has more authority, for he rules over more people."[5] He does not insult Achilles by doubting his divine parentage, as Agamemnon had, but he insists on the same point. Agamemnon has greater preponderance because his kingdom is larger. The size of his empire, not the massiveness of his fist, exacts obedience.

Homer seems to have arranged the catalogue in accordance with the conflict of Achilles and Agamemnon. Odysseus holds the center, just as he does

1. *Iliad* 1. 226–228.
2. *Ibid*. 2. 239–241.
3. *Ibid*. 1. 178.
4. *Ibid*. 1. 185–186, cf. 169.
5. *Ibid*. 1. 280–281; cf. 11. 786–787; *Odyssey* 15. 533–534.

in the camp,[6] but Ajax and Achilles, who occupy the camp's extreme wings, are here out of place. There are fourteen groups on either side of Odysseus: Achilles and Agamemnon are equally six places away from him. The number of ships is far greater on Agamemnon's than on Achilles' side (732 to 442); so that Homer emphasizes the wealth rather than the prowess which surrounds Agamemnon (placenames are double those on Achilles' side, and even the epithets suggest prosperity); while he neglects to list the cities of Achilles' partisans and recounts instead stories about the heroes themselves. We learn why Thoas is leader of the Aetolians, why Tlepolemus came from Rhodes, why Nireus brought so few ships, why Achilles stayed away from the war, how Protesilaus died, and why Philoctetes is absent:[7] but with Agamemnon none of the commanders are replacements and little is said about any of them. Thus the catalogue itself reflects the individual power of Achilles and the ancestral authority of Agamemnon.[8]

The catalogue is also intended to recover Agamemnon's prestige, which Achilles' attack had so greatly damaged: as if the number of his ships and of his followers would blot out his poor showing in front of Achilles, and dazzle us into acceptance of his sovereignty. Zeus also is willing, at least for a single day, to help out Nestor's plan, making Agamemnon tower over the many and superior to the heroes: "He excelled all the heroes because he was the best and led the most people."[9] Yet no one contested Achilles when he stated that he was the best, and that Agamemnon could only boast (or pray for) such a distinction.[10] And Homer's agreement, in the catalogue, with that boast is only a sop to Agamemnon's real humiliation: for no sooner has this providential superiority consoled him, than it is taken away: the Muses tell us that Ajax was the best as long as blameless Achilles remained angry.[11] For this reason Ajax, in the catalogue proper, is only given a line or two,[12] and his own excellence with the spear is assigned to his namesake Oilean Ajax, who is much smaller than himself and thus no rival to Agamemnon.[13]

Helen, ignorant of the dispute in the first book, sees Agamemnon enhanced by the catalogue, and unconsciously takes his part. In pointing him out to Priam – "That is Atreides, wide-ruling Agamemnon, who is both a good

6. *Iliad.* 2. 631–637; 11. 5–9.
7. *Ibid.* 2. 641–643, 657–670, 673–675, 687–694, 698–703, 721–725.
8. Odysseus' ships are the only ones called *miltoparêioi,* "red cheeked," (2. 637), an indication to the hearers that his position is central (cf. Eustathius *ad loc.*); and likewise the importance of Achilles is indicated by *nun au* (681, cf. Eustathius).
9. *Iliad* 2. 579–580, cf. 481–483, Eustathius *ad loc.*
10. Cf. *Iliad* 1. 91 with 244, 2. 82.
11. *Iliad* 2. 768–770, cf. 769, 7. 289.
12. *Ibid.* 2. 557–558.
13. *Ibid.* 2. 527–530.

King and a strong warrior" – [14] she assigns him the virtues Achilles had claimed for himself and denied to Agamemnon. Helen settles everything in Agamemnon's favor, giving him power and authority, which Diomedes, after the Achaeans have suffered great losses, could not possibly bring himself to admit. It is impetuous Diomedes, susceptible to Achilles' rhetoric, who finally declares Agamemnon's weakness: "The son of Cronus gave you the sceptre to be honored above all others, but he did not give you strength which is the greatest power."[15] Why Diomedes, however, can say in the ninth book what had caused the rift between Agamemnon and Achilles in the first, we must postpone answering until later.

Diomedes himself in the fifth book gives us the best example of ancestral virtue; and if we look at the first hundred lines, we can understand both its strength and its weakness: how it is the main source of his prowess and, for that very reason, how inadequate it is by itself. Athena begins by putting strength and boldness into "Tydeides Diomedes."[16] Diomedes and his father are almost identical. For over one hundred lines, while he works destruction everywhere – it is even unclear whose side he is on – [17] Diomedes' own name never recurs. He acts bravely and hence in the name of his father.[18] But when Sthenelus draws out the arrow with which Pandarus had wounded him, and the blood spurts through his shirt of mail, as Diomedes, not as Tydeides, he prays to Athena.[19] His paternal impetus once checked, he must summon help in his own name: he begs Athena to stand by him even as she once stood by his father.[20] Athena responds, calls him simply "Diomedes," and promises aid. Thus restored to favor, he becomes once again Tydeides.[21] Diomedes as an individual is weak, but as the son of his father he is irresistible. Not in himself but in his lineage, of which he is very conscious,[22] resides most of his own greatness. It is ironic, however, that it should be Diomedes, a hero so narrowly bound to the past, who challenges the authority of Agamemnon.

Agamemnon, as we have seen, knows how important ancestry is. When he wishes to rebuke Diomedes, who has not yet rejected his right to do so, he praises his father's courage and slights his own; and Athena herself incites Diomedes by the same argument, concluding: "Therefore you are not the off-

---

14. *Ibid.* 3. 178–179.
15. *Ibid.* 9. 37–39; cf. 1. 231, 293.
16. *Ibid.* 5. 1.
17. *Ibid.* 5. 86.
18. *Ibid.* 5. 16, 18, 25. 85, 93, 97.
19. *Ibid.* 5. 114.
20. *Ibid.* 5. 116–117.
21. *Ibid.* 5. 134.
22. *Ibid.* 14. 110–127.

spring of Tydeus, warlike Oeneides."[23] Athena, in denying that Diomedes is
the son of Tydeus, says at the same time that Tydeus was the son of Oeneus.
Not to be the son of one's father is the greatest shame; to surpass one's father
unthinkable. When Sthenelus attempts to rank Diomedes and himself above
their fathers, Diomedes silences him.[24] One must be content with "ancestral
strength," which Athena in fact grants Diomedes; beyond that a hero cannot
go.[25] Yet Odysseus, far from imitating his father, calls himself after
Telemachus;[26] for he is not only, in a sense, the author of himself but the
author of another. He is the beginning of a new line.[27]

The absence of Achilles makes Agamemnon more and more aware of his
false position; so that he is at last forced to concede him everything except a
superiority in age, upon which he now bases his greater royalty.[28] It is a concession, however, which Odysseus, in repeating Agamemnon's promises to
Achilles, prudently omits.[29]

After the embassy fails, Agamemnon's despair increases still further. He
fears that Diomedes might pick, as his companion on a night patrol,
Menelaus: "Nor you in shame leave behind the better, and yielding to shame
choose the worse, looking at a lineage, not even if the worse is more royal."[30]
Diomedes' sense of shame must not interfere with his knowledge. He must
judge Menelaus stripped of his titles, which is so much easier to do under the
cover of night. Agamemnon now affirms, what he just as strongly before
denied, that rank and birth are no guarantee of virtue. He realizes now how
wrong he had been; it takes Achilles much longer to acknowledge his guilt.

At the funeral games the struggle between innate and inherited virtue
reappears. It is staged for Achilles' benefit. Menelaus becomes very angry
with Antilochus, because he had tricked him into yielding his advantage. The
trick made him third instead of second: "You have shamed my virtue *aretê*,
you have blasted my horses, putting your own in front, which you know are
much worse . . . [Let the Argives judge between us], lest one of them say,

---

23. Ibid. 4. 370–400; 5. 812–813. It is not accidental that Agamemnon alone calls
    Odysseus "Laertiades," without adding his proper name (19. 185); nor that he
    bids Menelaus "call each man by his lineage and patronytnic, glorifying all" (10.
    68–69; cf. 5. 635–639; 7. 125–128; 8. 282–283). Nicias, Thucydides'
    Agamemnon, does the same (vii. 69. 2.), Cf. Xenophon *Oeconomicus* vii. 3.
24. *Ibid.* 4. 404–412.
25. *Ibid.* 5. 125; cf. 6. 479; 15. 641–642; *Odyssey* 2. 276–277; Horace C. i.xv. 27–28.
26. *Iliad.* 4. 354; 2. 260.
27. Cf. Meyer. *de Homeri patronymicis,* pp. 61–66, who points out the rarity of
    patronymics in the *Odyssey*: but he wrongly infers from this its more recent ori-
    gin, whereas it actually indicates the intended difference between the two works.
28. *Iliad* 9. 160–161, cf. 69.
29. Cf. *Iliad* 9. 392.
30. *Iliad* 10. 237–239.

Menelaus by lies and by force worsted Antilochus, and he takes the horse as his prize, because his horses were much worse, but he himself stronger, in virtue and strength *(aretêi te biêi te)*."[31] It has been usual to translate *arete* differently each time: first as skill, then as dignity:[32] but the point is lost unless Menelaus refers twice to the same virtue. "Better" has as its correlate "worse": the horses of Menelaus will be thought worse, and Menelaus himself better, in "virtue and strength." Menelaus would on the one hand be lying, if he said his horses were better and they were not,[33] and on the other he would be using "virtue and strength" to gain the prize. Menelaus can mean only one thing by virtue:

> *Est in iuvencis, est in equis patrum virtus*
> (There is in bullocks, there is in horses, the virtue of their fathers).

Virtue and lineage are for Menelaus interchangeable. "You have shamed my virtue," he says, but he means his family. "The Achaeans will say my horses were inferior in virtue and strength, while I won by superior virtue and strength": Menelaus means in both cases family. As his horses are good, so are they of good family: as he himself is of good family, so is he virtuous. Family and virtue are the same. Laertes in the *Odyssey* similarly confounds them. Odysseus begs Telemachus not to shame the race of his fathers, and after Telemachus promises he will not, Laertes, who has overheard them, rejoices because "his son and his grandson contested about virtue."[34] Laertes and Menelaus are agreed: a virtue always descends from father to son. But what we would call skill (namely, Antilochus' device for getting ahead), and what Nestor calls "craft," Menelaus can only think of as guile.[35] Virtue is family, art is base deception. Menelaus reunites what Achilles had taken apart: he holds, like Agamemnon, the sceptre while speaking.[36]

31. *Ibid*. 23. 571–585.
32. So Leaf *ad* 571.
33. *Iliad* 23. 572.
34. *Odyssey* 24. 508–515, cf. *Iliad* 6. 209–211; Pindar *Nemean* xi. 37–38.
35. *Iliad* 23. 322, 515, 585, cf. 415.
36. *Ibid*. 23, 568, cf. 587–588; 1. 260; 2. 707.

Chapter V
The Armor of Agamemnon

Many readers must have noticed that Agamemnon, though he plays a great part in the *Iliad,* possesses few epithets. His honorifics scarcely match his honor. He is regularly adorned with five: Menelaus can claim at least twelve. But were these five peculiar to himself, perhaps they would prove no less illustrious for being few. This however is not the case. *Anax andrôn,* "lord of men," he is allowed to enjoy by himself, until we meet the enemy and find that Anchises and Aeneas also have it;[1] or Nestor, in his garrulity, bestows it on Augeias.[2] These somehow may be thought worthy enough to be ranked with Agamemnon: but when Euphetes, about whom nothing is known, and worse still Eumelus, an Achaean who led but eleven ships, obtain it,[3] Agamemnon's glory is stolen from him. Likewise he shares *poimên laôn,* "shepherd of the people," not only with Dryas, whom Nestor numbers among the former great, but with the obscure Bias, Hypeiron, and Thrasymedes.[4] It is even twice applied to his enemy Achilles.[5] *Dios,* "brilliant," needs no comment, for it adorns almost all heroes. Only *eury kreiôn,* wide-ruling, which Poseidon once usurps,[6] and *kydistos,* "most glorious," which often describes Zeus, may be considered Agamemnon's own. His consolation, of course, may be that others are called "shepherd of the people" or "lord of men" only on special occasions, while he constantly enjoys them: but these few occasions are sufficient to lower his rank. Having so few distinctions, he must be more jealous of their use than Achilles, who, in the abundance of his store, can afford to be prodigal.[7]

To marshal his troops Agamemnon's epithets suffice: but to wage war with them would be folly. The enemy cannot be expected to consider, in the

1. *Iliad* 5. 268, 311.
2. *Ibid.* 11. 701.
3. *Ibid.* 15. 532; 23. 288 cf. 2. 713.
4. *Ibid.* 1. 263; 4. 296; 5. 144; 9. 81.
5. *Ibid.* 16. 2; 19. 386.
6. *Ibid.* 11.751.
7. Achilles bears approximately 28 epithets, Hector 17, Odysseus 12, Menelaus 13, Ajax 17; and of them Odysseus alone has several that are shared with no one else, mostly compounds with *poly-*.

midst of battle, the extent of his sway. He stands almost naked for the business of war: he must be armed, before entering it, more carefully than anyone else. His arming of himself begins his *aristeia*. Piece by piece Agamemnon is put together and made a hero. The effort is so great that Athena and Hera must make "loud clamor in order to honor the king of wealthy Mycenae."[8] His careful fitting contrasts sharply with Hector, who needs no time to arm himself, but he is shown at once bearing his shield among the front ranks.[9] Moreover, Hector fires the imagination of Homer: his essence can be caught in a simile: he is like a baleful star, sometimes flashing through the clouds, sometimes ducking behind them.[10] But Agamemnon cannot be fused into a single image: he remains in fragments. His armor clothes, it does not transform him. It is his breastplate, not himself, that calls for a simile, whose snakes gleam "like the rainbow Zeus sticks in a cloud, a portent for mankind."[11] Not Agamemnon but his breastplate is more than the sum of its parts; not Agamemnon but his well-wrought shield is "furious."[12] Though the bronze of his armor flashed far into the heavens, the wonder of it fails to impress us: we suspect that Hera and Athena have intervened. The statement is too literal. He is unpoetic. But Hector's bronze "shone like the lightning of Father Zeus the aegis-bearer."[13] His armor is as miraculous as his own person.

Armor makes the man: it covers his fears and his cowardice. When Paris agrees to fight Menelaus, he dons his armor, as the husband of fair-haired Helen, just as methodically as Agamemnon. Indeed, his breastplate is borrowed, and, Homer adds, "he adjusted it to fit himself."[14] And having completed Paris, as it were, Homer does not go through it again for Menelaus; who, though not much of a warrior, is so much better than Paris, that it suffices to say, "so in the same way warlike Menelaus put on his armor."[15] Menelaus is already armed with his epithet "warlike"; but Paris needs more protection than the epithet "godlike" *(theoeidês)* can afford.

Nestor and Odysseus find Diomedes sleeping outside his tent, still clothed in all of his armor, while his companions rest their heads on their shields.[16] Not even in sleep can Diomedes the man peel off Diomedes the warrior. Man means: armed man. Armor is a promise of power; it is, like a hero's patronymic, a proof of his eminence. If he is deprived of this emblem, which is sometimes handed down from his father, he might be mistaken for a com-

8.   *Iliad* 11. 45–46.
9.   *Ibid.* 11. 61.
10.   *Ibid.* 11. 62–63.
11.   *Ibid.* 11. 27–28.
12.   *Ibid.* 11. 32.
13.   *Ibid.* 11. 65–66.
14.   *Ibid.* 3. 333.
15.   *Ibid.* 3. 339; cf. 10. 121–123; 17. 588.
16.   *Ibid.* 10. 150–152.

mon warrior and lose his claim to ancestral virtue.[17] When Hector thinks of appealing to Achilles, having taken off his helmet, laid down his shield, and rested his spear against a wall, he suddenly stops himself: "He will kill me even though I am naked and as if I were a woman."[18] A hero becomes like a woman and thinks of himself as naked, as soon as he is deprived of spear, helmet and shield.[19] Not the force in his limbs but the force in his armor transmutes a man into a hero. He acts as if he were the instrument of his own weapons and subject to them. How elaborately the Achaeans prepare in the Doloneia, merely to attend a meeting! Agamemnon puts on a coat of mail and takes a spear; Nestor does the same; and neither helmeted Menelaus nor armed Diomedes forgets his spear.[20] Only Odysseus forgets and takes but a shield: for his part in the patrol is defensive, and Diomedes does the killing.[21]

When Patroclus is stripped of Achilles' armor, Achilles knows that he cannot go into battle unarmed, and yet he feels that the armor of no one else would suit him: only the shield of Ajax would accord with his dignity,[22] as if the arms of another would make him lose his own identity.[23] When Zeus, on the other hand, fitted the arms of Achilles to Hector, at once great Ares crept into him, and his limbs were filled with strength."[24] Zeus no doubt partly inspires him, but it is equally the arms themselves, made by Hephaestus, that lend him support. Here is not just the flash of bronze, which dazzles the enemy and leaves him unchanged: but here is an inner sympathy between Hector and his armor that creates a single implement of war. Even the heroes acknowledge the partial identity of arms and the man, *arma virumque*.[25] Pandarus speaks thus to Aeneas, when he asks him who the Achaean warrior is who slays so many Trojans: "I liken him in all respects to warlike Tydeides, knowing him by his shield and his helmet, and seeing his horses."[26] Diomedes is known by his shield, his horses, and his helmet. To lose them would be to lose the best part of himself,[27] so that every hero is as intent on capturing pieces of armor as he is on killing their owner: for should he fail to despoil his victim, he has no record of the deed. Trophies bear witness to his prowess: they guarantee his fame.

Patroclus fills perfectly the armor of Achilles, and when he first appears,

17. Cf. Iliad 17. 191–197.
18. *Iliad* 22. 124–125; cf. *Odyssey* 10. 300–301.
19. Cf. *Iliad* 21. 50.
20. *Iliad* 10. 21–24. 31. 131–135, 178; cf. 29–30 with 3. 17.
21. *Ibid.* 10. 149; cf. BT Scholiast.
22. *Ibid.* 18. 192–195.
23. Cf. Vergil *Aen.* ii. 396.
24. *Iliad* 17. 210–212; cf. 19. 384–386.
25. Xenophon *Anabasis* ii. i. 12.
26. *Iliad* 5. 181–183.
27. Cf. *Iliad* 7. 424; 11. 613–614.

he is mistaken for him;[28] but it is his inability to wield Achilles' spear that tells the difference between them.[29] Had Patroclus been able to wield it, we would have had two Achilles.

28. *Iliad* 16. 278–282.
29. *Ibid.* 16. 141–144; cf. Eustathius *ad* 140.

Chapter VI
Ajax

Nireus was the most beautiful man, after Achilles, who came to Troy; but he was weak and few people followed him.[1] Lacking both the ancestral authority of Agamemnon and the inborn power of Achilles, he showed up so poorly in the war that, outside the catalogue, he never is mentioned. That beauty does not carry with it any strength, we know already from Paris;[2] but strength can yet draw a man into beauty. Although Ajax at first is only the best warrior among the Achaeans after Achilles,[3] he assumes, in the stress and strain of war, when the Trojans are about to drag away Patroclus' corpse, a greater likeness to him: "Ajax, who in beauty as in deeds surpassed all the Danaans except the son of Peleus."[4] His deeds shed a lustre over his appearance, so that he usurps the place of Nireus, whose peacetime beauty counts as nothing in battle.[5] The parents of Nireus gave him a superficial beauty, that reflected, as it were, the glorious bravery of their own names (Aglaie and Charopus: "Splendor" and "Flash"), but that yielded to brute Ajax in the shock of war.

We know the war-mettle of Ajax before Achilles', and that he imperfectly copies heroic virtue; but his very imperfection serves as our only possible guide to Achilles. Were we to witness Achilles' valor in the seventh book, instead of Ajax', we could form no just idea of his greatness: but after having before us his inferior, though he is apparently flawless, the peculiar virtues of Achilles become something clear and precise.

> He doth permit the base contagious clouds
> To smother up his beauty from the world,
> That, when he please again to be himself,
> Being wanted, he may be more wonder'd at,

1. *Iliad* 2. 671–675; cf. Aristotle *Rhetoric* 1414a2–7; Lucian *Dial*. xxv.
2. But cf. *Iliad* 6. 522.
3. *Iliad* 2. 768.
4. *Ibid.* 17. 279–280.
5. Cf. *Iliad* 6. 156, where Bellerophon has "lovely manliness," *ênoreên erateinên*, a unique collocation: *erateinên* is used of a country or Helen's daughter *(Iliad* 3. 175, 239, 401; *Odyssey* 4. 13) and *ênoreê* of strength *(Iliad* 4. 303; 11. 9; 17. 329; *Odyssey* 24. 509).

By breaking through the foul and ugly mists
Of vapors that did seem to strangle him.

We must look then more closely at Ajax. A hundred lines of the eleventh
book, in which he displays more of himself than elsewhere, are the best place
to begin. The Trojans have tracked down the wounded Odysseus; and Ajax,
summoned by Menelaus, enters the fray, as is his custom, without a word.[6]
Homer aptly compares him to a lion, who chases off jackals from a stag: "then
devours it himself."[7] These last words seem not only inexact (common enough
in similes) but inapplicable: for Ajax has come to defend and not to kill
Odysseus. Yet Homer wished to indicate, in the aside of his simile, that Ajax'
excellence does not include his loyalty. He is a warrior first, an Achaean second: he could have been as readily a Trojan.[8]

Ajax is all head and shoulders, and carries his shield like a turret: even in
motion he seems to stand still.[9] He plays a large part in the defense of the wall:
when its tower is threatened, Menestheus prefers him before others; and
Teucer, just as if Ajax were a battlement, shoots his arrows from behind him
and his shield.[10]

As Ajax wounds one Trojan after another, Homer likens him to a river
swollen by winter rains: "Many flourishing oaks and many pines it carries
away, and casts much trash into the sea."[11] The river sweeps away not only
oaks and pines (trees to which falling warriors are often compared) but trash:
so Ajax wounded Lysandrus and Pyrasus, whose names occur nowhere else;
and Pylartes, whom Patroclus later killed; and even his noblest victim,
Doryclus the son of Priam, is illegitimate.[12] He lacks discrimination in his
slaughter of horses and men.[13]

Ajax is hard-pressed but retreats reluctantly, like a lion driven away from
cattle. The simile would have little point (it is used elsewhere of Menelaus),[14]
were it not for what follows: an ass he seems, glutted on corn, whom children
beat out of a field.[15] He is a beast (*thêr*), the word Homer employs in bringing together these two similes.[16] Aristotle must have had this passage in mind,

6. *Iliad* 11. 465–472; cf. his silence in Book 10 and 3. 292.
7. *Ibid*. 11. 474–481; cf. 15. 271–280 of Hector; Aristotle *HA* 610a13–14. More than
   any other Achaean, Ajax (in Homer's eyes) is a lion: *Iliad* 7. 256; 11. 548–557;
   13. 197–202; 17. 132–137; cf. Plato *Republic* 620b1–2.
8. Cf. *Iliad* 11. 570–571.
9. *Iliad* 3. 227; 7. 219; 11. 485; 17. 128; cf. 11. 526–527.
10. *Ibid*. 12. 330–350; 8. 266–268; cf. 17. 121–137.
11. *Ibid*. 11. 494–495.
12. *Ibid*. 11. 489–490.
13. *Ibid*. 11. 496–497.
14. *Ibid*. 11. 548–557; 17. 656–667.
15. *Ibid*. 11. 558–562, cf. 67–69, its source.
16. *Ibid*. 11: 546.

when after showing how Homer made Hector and Diomedes possess a kind of noble courage, he continues: "Honor and the noble incite the brave to action, and spirit (*thymos*) works with them; but pain incites animals, . . . who are not courageous, since pain and spirit alone goad them to face dangers they fail to foresee; for even asses, if they are hungry, would be brave, and, though they are beaten, refuse to budge from pasture."[17] Whatever nobility, then, Ajax has, he shares with Menelaus (it is of the most general kind): but what makes him unique, his stubbornness, lacks all nobility. He is a glutton in war: insatiate.[18]

When Ajax is called the best, after Achilles, both in deeds and in beauty, he is at once compared to a wild boar, an animal which Achilles himself never seems to imitate.[19] Ajax after all, Homer admits, even if ennobled by war, is quite ugly. In short, as lion, boar, and ass, we may call him: *thymôdês* ("quick-tempered") but *eleutherios* ("noble"), *enstatikos* ("ferocious") but *andreios* ("courageous"), *amathes* ("unmanageable") but *eugenês* ("well-born").[20]

---

17.   Aristotle *EN* 1116a21–35, 1116b30–1117a1.
18.   *Iliad* 12. 335.
19.   *Ibid.* 17. 281–283.
20.   Cf. Aristotle *HA* 488b15–17.

Chapter VII
Heroic Virtue

"To no man would Telamonian Ajax yield . . . nor would he retreat before Achilles the man-smasher, if they fought hand-to-hand; but in swiftness he cannot rival him."[1] Idomeneus very exactly describes Ajax thus: only in swiftness does Achilles excel him, for in pitched battle Ajax would be his equal. Achilles is better than Ajax because he is faster, and if we wish to find someone like him in this respect, we need only look to Ajax' namesake: "Ajax slew the most, the fast son of Oileus; for no one was his equal in following up a rout, whenever Zeus put fear into them."[2] Speed is needed to follow up a rout, bulkiness to cover a retreat. That two men, who would almost match Achilles if combined (they often appear together), should bear the same name is a brilliant stroke.[3] Achilles is Telamonian, added to Oilean, Ajax: the shoulders belong to one, the legs to the other.[4] We see in each of them separately some of Achilles' vices which, because he contains both their virtues, are in himself concealed.

We have come round at last to Achilles' most frequent epithet, "swift-footed," which seems to occur in such reckless profusion throughout the *Iliad;* but Homer manages its use more finely than many suppose. Although swiftness of foot does not in itself sum up all virtues, for ugly Dolon has it (*hos dê toi eidos men eên kakos, alla podôkês,* – "who was ill-favored in looks, but swift-footed"),[5] yet, if someone is more beautiful than Nireus and as bulky as Ajax,[6] it suffices to set him apart from all others.[7] It seals the doom of Hector when he tries to flee.[8] It is the most obvious proof of Achilles' power, so that even his eloquence seems based upon it. He assumes it first when he addresses Agamemnon: swift-footed Achilles is pitted against the son of Atreus.[9] It

1.   *Iliad* 13. 321-325.
2.   *Ibid.* 14. 520–522.
3.   Cf. *Iliad* 17. 718–721.
4.   Cf. *Iliad* 13. 71–79.
5.   *Iliad* 10. 316.
6.   *Iliad.* 2. 671–675; 21.527; 22. 92; cf. 5. 395; 7. 208.
7.   Cf. Livy ix. 16. 11–19.
8.   *Iliad* 22. 161.
9.   *Ibid.* 1. 54. 58.

assures Calchas, uncertain whether he may speak the truth or not: it convinces him that Achilles is stronger than Atreides, and hence he has nothing to fear.[10] And Achilles, as long as he irritates Agamemnon (illustrating in his speech his power), is swift-footed, but when Athena persuades him not to use his strength, and he replaces his sword in its sheath, he becomes "Peleides."[11] His piety, gaining for the moment the upper hand, lets him reassume his father's name.

Achilles receives the epithet "swift-footed" more than any other man, but one animal has it almost as often. Horses are *ôkypodes*. They resemble Achilles in his proudest virtue, and only if we discover how the horse and the hero are related, shall we see Achilles in a true perspective. The word *aretê*, "virtue," occurs, all told, sixteen times in the *Iliad*.[12] It is used exclusively of horses and men.[13] But what is equine virtue? "A horse must be both strong and beautiful: its strength resides in the legs, its beauty in the head."[14] Thus it is the perfect image for Achilles, the swiftest and most beautiful of the heroes. What is more Aristotle assigns to the horse two virtues (among others) which, we have seen, characterize Achilles: "The virtue of a horse makes him both run quickly and abide the enemy."[15] It is, therefore, right and proper that Achilles should have the best horses.[16]

That Achilles harmoniously unites two virtues that usually cannot even fit together, stamina and speed, constitutes the miracle of his excellence; for what Lady Wentworth says of racehorses, that "it is doubtful whether extreme sprinting speed can be combined with extreme staying power" – no less doubtful than that "a weight-lifter [can be] built like an acrobat"[17] – holds true for heroic virtue. Oilean Ajax is much smaller than his namesake;[18] but Achilles did not sacrifice the swiftness of one to acquire the turret-like stolidity of the other. He is, in a real sense, more than the sum of his parts.

Paris dons his armor and comes to join the fight. Homer describes him brilliantly: "And he, when he had put on his famous armor, curiously wrought in bronze, rushed through the city, confident in his swift feet: as when some stabled horse, fed in its stall, breaks its bonds and rushes over the plain, strik-

---

10. *Ibid.* 1. 84. cf. 80.
11. *Ibid.* 1. 121, 148 (cf. 215). 223–224.
12. *Ibid.* 8. 535; 11. 90; 13. 237, 275, 277; 14. 118 (cf. 15. 642); 20. 242, 411; 22. 268. 11. 763 and 9. 498 are used of Achilles; 23. 276, 374 of horses; cf. Pindar *Pythian* x. 23; Herodotus iii. 88. 3, i. 216; *Iliad* 20. 411 refers only to swiftness.
13. *Iliad* 9. 498 is an apparent exception.
14. Theomnestus in *Hippiatrica Cant.* xciii. 93 (ed. Oder-Hoppe).
15. Aristotle *EN* 1106a19–21; cf. *Iliad* 5. 222–223. 230–234; 10. 491–493; 18. 808–809; *Odyssey* 4. 202.
16. *Iliad* 2. 769-770.
17. *British Horses and Ponies,* pp. 23–24.
18. *Iliad* 2. 527–529.

ing the earth with his hooves, accustomed to bathe in the fair-flowing river, rejoicing: it holds its head high, and its mane streams from the shoulders (confident in its splendor), its swift legs bring it to the pastures and the herd of horses: so the son of Priam, Paris, brilliant in his arms, came like the sun from the top of Pergamun, smiling with self-satisfaction, and his swift legs brought him."[19] Critics have been annoyed that Hector obtains the same simile – "So Apollo said and breathed strength into the shepherd of his people, as when etc." – [20] and yet the reason for the repetition is not hard to find. Both are equally swift but exultant differently. Paris, godlike in his beauty, flashing like the sun and "smiling with self-satisfaction,"[21] puts on beautiful armor; while Hector returns to the fight, after being almost mortally wounded, with renewed strength. Paris is beautiful like Nireus, Hector like Ajax: even in war Paris has the glitter of peace, even in a lull Hector terrifies his son.[22] Paris' brilliance will fade in battle, Hector's force will increase. They stand at the two poles of heroic excellence, beauty and power, which are fused in Achilles (and only these three heroes are compared to horses): "As a triumphant horse with his chariot rushes, who easily in the stretch runs over the plain, so Achilles managed his swift feet and knees."[23] Achilles then is a mixture, among the Achaeans, of the two Ajax; among the Trojans, of Paris and Hector.

This general resemblance of men and horses Homer pursues even to small particulars. He tells us what is the most fatal spot for horse and man alone (they are not the same);[24] and he implies that, in the eyes of the gods there is no difference between the providence extended to horses and men: Zeus pities the immortal horses of Achilles, who weep for Patroclus, even as he pities Hector, prancing in the arms of Achilles.[25] Achilles' arms and Achilles' horses would be the two greatest prizes for Hector.[26] That he captures one, while the other eludes him, spells out his doom. Zeus allowed him the one and refused him the other: mortal Patroclus he can kill, Xanthus and Balius he cannot. Achilles survives to kill him, they to humiliate his corpse.

Virtue shows itself in foot and hand: to have both in the highest degree is to be Achilles. Yet virtue consists in another element which Achilles is slow to demonstrate: the willingness to use what one has. Horses have it almost everywhere: (*tô ouk aekonte petesthên* – but not unwillingly the two flew forward.")[27] Obedience to the lash of his driver suffices for a horse; but in the

---

19. *Ibid.* 6. 504–514, cf. 513 with 19. 398.
20. *Ibid.* 15. 262–270 (264–268 = 6. 507–511).
21. So Leaf *ad Iliad* 6. 514; cf. 3. 43; 11. 378.
22. *Iliad* 6. 466–470, cf. 318–322.
23. *Ibid.* 22. 22–24, cf. 162–165.
24. *Ibid.* 8. 83–84. 325–326; it is curious that Paris should hit the horse, Hector the man; cf. 22. 324–325; 8. 85; 13. 568–569.
25. *Ibid.* 17. 198–208, 441–450; consider 8. 186–190; cf. Eustathius *ad* 188–189.
26. Cf. *Iliad* 10. 305–306, 322–323, 402–404 (= 17. 76–78).

case of a hero, though he sometimes fails to realize it, his obedience must come from within. Willingness must accompany a hero's knowledge and efficiency. Hence only the Achaeans as a body, and never the Trojans (who defend themselves by necessity),[28] fight with *aretê*.[29]

Eumaeus complains to Odysseus that nothing runs smoothly any more, ever since his master went away; not even the dog Argus was cared for: "And the servants, as soon as their masters no longer stand over them, are unwilling to do what they ought; for half of virtue Zeus takes away from a man, when the day of slavery overtakes him."[30] A man does not lose in slavery his skill but his willingness to perform *enaisima* ("just things" – with the sense of having been decreed by the gods), which are the things one should do if one knows them. "No one who is just," says Hector to Paris, "would ever blame your work in battle, since you are strong; but willingly you hold off and do not wish to fight."[31] To be strong is not enough: one must wish to use one's strength: one must be willing to die.[32]

27. *Ibid.* 5. 366, 768; 8. 45; 10. 530; 11. 281, 519; 22. 400; but cf. 23. 446–447.
28. *Ibid.* 8. 56–57; cf. 24. 668.
29. *Ibid.* 11. 90; 13. 237.
30. *Odyssey* 17. 320–323.
31. *Iliad* 6. 521–523; cf. 13. 117–119.
32. Cf. *Iliad* 4. 224, 297–300; 13. 232–234; Aristotle *EN* 1115a32–35, 1115b4–5.

Chapter VIII
Achilles and Hector

When Hector sees Paris retreating before Menelaus' advance, he rebukes him sharply; Paris humbly submits but, almost as an aside, complains of Hector's ruthlessness: "Your heart is always like an unwearying axe, by which a man cuts through a ship's plank with the help of his art *(technê),* and the axe increases his force *(erôên)*."[1] Paris' simile is unique in many ways. Nowhere else is a hero compared to a man-made thing; nor does the word *technê* recur in the *Iliad* (common enough though it is in the *Odyssey*);[2] nor is *erôê* used commonly of a man but of a spear's cast.[3] Hector is not the woodsman but the axe, or rather woodsman and axe; his heart multiplies his strength; he is self-sufficient. He carries within himself the means to greater power. He is all weapon.

Hector does not stand alone in being a mere instrument of himself. *Nêlês,* "merciless," often describes two things: to avoid death is to ward off *nêlees êmar,* a merciless day; to be slain is sometimes to be cut *nêleï chalkôi,* with merciless bronze.[4] A day of death is merciless but perhaps bronze would be better called indifferent. Yet Achilles and no one else is *nêlês.*[5] His spirit is iron.[6] He is a thing, indifferent and merciless: as inevitable as death; as unfeeling as bronze. "Made by some other divinity than nature," Hector and Achilles embody the ultimate ambition of a hero: to be no man at all.

1. *Iliad* 3. 60–63.
2. Cf. *Iliad* 23. 415.
3. *Iliad* 4. 542; 15. 358; 21. 251; 23. 529; 14. 488 of a man.
4. W. Schulze, *Qusestiones Epicicae,* pp. 289–290, derives *nelees* of *nelees êmar* from *aleomai* ("shun"), and E. Risch, *Wortbildung der Homerischen Sprache,* p. 76. n. 1, thinks both adjectives may come originally from *aleomai,* but that later both were derived from *eleos* ("pity"). In any case, Homer, I think, did not distinguish them.
5. *Iliad* 9. 497, 632; 16. 33, 204; cf. 19. 229; Pindar *Pythian* I. 95–96.
6. *Ibid.* 22. 357. If we set aside its occurrence in lists (e.g., 5. 723), iron mostly indicates horror, savagery, or indifference: 4. 123, 510; 7 141, 144; 8. 15; 17. 424, 565; 18. 34; 22. 357; 23. 30; cf. *Odyssey* 16. 294. Iron and bronze are related one to the other in Homer like steel and gold in Shakespeare's line: "To lift shrewd steel against our golden crown" *(Richard II* 3. 2. 59).

> That for Achilles' image stood his spear
> Gripped in an armed hand; himself behind
> Was left unseen, save to the eye of mind:
>   A hand, a foot, a face, a leg, a head.
>   Stood for the whole to be imagined.[7]

Patroclus, who understands Achilles, begs him to return to the war; and feeling, while he speaks, that Achilles stiffens himself to refuse him, denies what seemed Achilles' inalienable possession: "Pitiless one, horseman Peleus was not your father, nor Thetis your mother; but the grey-green sea and steep rocks bore you, for your mind is harsh."[8] Thetis and Peleus could never have been the parents of Achilles: sea and rocks must have begot him. Patroclus has chosen his image carefully. Achilles' mother, instead of being a Nereid, is the sea itself; and Achilles' father, instead of being a grandson of Zeus, is a fabulous rock. "Tell me your ancestry," Penelope says to the disguised Odysseus, "for you are not from fabled oak or rock."[9] Achilles' divine lineage, known to be but three generations, becomes uncountable and formless. He is as anonymous as Odysseus.

If we compare Patroclus' bitter words with a similar passage, Achilles' uniqueness will appear more clearly. Hector cannot break through the lines of Achaeans who defend the ships, holding him back "like a great steep rock, set near the iron-grey sea, that resists the swift onrush of shrill winds and foaming waves, which break, crash and roar against it."[10] The Trojans as waves and winds beat vainly against the Achaeans, a steep rock. Achilles may seem at first, as the offspring of rock and sea, to be nothing more than "half-Trojan and half-Greek": but he is more. Achilles is what others only seem to be. Whereas the Achaeans and Trojans are rock and sea by Homer's fiat, their identity to be changed as the scene itself changes, Achilles' character is more permanent. He is the son, however unnatural, of sea and stone, and as such beyond the whims of Homer. The harshness of Achilles resides in his elemental lineage, that of the Achaeans and Trojans in a likeness; just as the mild temper of Patroclus, when he beseeches Achilles, is shown in his weeping like a spring, "which pours its dark waters down a precipice."[11] Patroclus' grief evokes a comparison in which he does not become, as Achilles does, the objects in the simile but merely resembles their outer appearance. Not abandoning himself in the image, he assumes only its manner; while Achilles is the very substance of Patroclus' aspect, as if the sea were the source of every

7.   Shakespeare *Rape of Lucrece* 1424–1428.
8.   *Iliad* 16. 33–35; cf. Aeschylus *Prometheus Bound* 242, 299–302.
9.   *Odyssey* 19. 162–163; cf. *Iliad* 21. 190–199; 22. 126–128.
10. *Iliad* 15. 618–621.
11. *Ibid.* 16. 3–4; cf. Eustathius 16. 31.

spring and the steep cliffs of every precipice. He is the reality that lies behind the accidental and the momentary, and hence he cannot change his being and his origins as others change their attributes. He wears no disguises.

Chapter IX
Similes

Hephaestus divided Achilles' shield into three parts: sky, earth and sea.[1] Sun, moon, and stars, which seem to make up the whole of heaven, are done in a few lines; and the sea, which surrounds the shield, even more quickly; but the earth, or rather man's business on earth, takes up most of Homer's description.[2] The city at war requires more time to depict than the city at peace: but the peaceful tasks of men predominate over both.[3]

Homer made the shield as an image of his two works, but his picture of war, the *Iliad,* is explained by similes taken over from the peaceful scenes of the shield; while his picture of peace, the *Odyssey,* merely repeats the same scene.[4] The ocean on which Odysseus travels is the real ocean, while the storms and tempests in the *Iliad* are borrowed images. War cannot explain itself. It needs to be glossed by peace. It is an abstract of peace, unable to make full use of its richness, so that the similes are restricted and, except for one detail, sometimes fail to correspond. Only the idea or sentiment that lies behind a simile can be shared with the bleakness of war.[5] Peace needs no similes, it is what everyone knows. A simile would merely duplicate our own vision and add nothing to it. War, the unfamiliar, must be shown in terms of the familiar, so that only through the *Odyssey* can we understand the *Iliad.* The simile puts the heroes in the perspective of peace, of what they resemble in the world around us. Indeed it is because war seems more desirable than peace – to stay at Troy more desirable than to return home – that Homer can use peaceful similes.[6] But can counterparts to the heroes be found in our world? or must peace be distorted to fit them? We must look more closely at the similes to find Homer's answer. The twelfth and thirteenth books are perhaps the clearest examples; for the heroes are restricted to the battlefield, so that the series of similes are uninterrupted and contribute to a single idea.

1. *Iliad* 18. 483; cf. 15. 187–193.
2. *Ibid.* 18. 483–489, 607–608.
3. *Ibid.* 18. 491–508, 509–540, 541–606; BT Scholiast 490.
4. Cf. *Iliad* 18. 550–557 with 11. 67–70; all the similes of lions are derived, as it were, from 18. 579–586; but see *Iliad* 18. 605–606 and *Odyssey* 4. 17–18; cf. *Odyssey* 4. 1–7 with *Iliad* 18. 491–496.
5. Cf. Fraenkel, *Dichtung and Philosophie der Frühen Griechentum,* pp. 58–59.
6. Cf. *Iliad* 2. 453–454; 11. 13–14.

What Hector is compared to at first sets up an opposition that Homer repeats and enlarges upon in the succeeding similes. Hector leads the charge like a lion and a whirlwind.[7] He is both animate and inanimate nature: animal and thing.[8] As a whirlwind he is absolute; his opponents are not described. As a boar or lion he becomes contentious and forms but part of the scene: hemmed in by dogs and huntsmen, his eyes gleaming with strength, the lion tries to make his way out, and not fear but rashness finally kills him.[9] As whirlwind, Hector is alone, and

> Runs rushing o'er the lines of men, as if 'twere
> A perpetual spoil;

as lion, Hector finds himself surrounded, his liberty chained to a narrow circle, within which he must move and die.

Then Asius makes his diversionary sally against the wall of the Achaeans, which Polypoetes and Leonteus, fixed like two oaks (their long roots unmoved by wind and rain), defend.[10] Here the whirlwind of Hector has become the wind and rain of Asius, who meets his first resistance in the oaken Lapiths. The absolute rush and motion of the winds encounter two oaks, which are, just as absolutely, obstinate and immobile. But as soon as they charge and engage in combat, they do not differ from the boarlike Hector. Now the Trojans under Asius are the dogs and huntsmen which the Achaeans before had represented.[11] The roles of attacker and defender are reversed, but the reversal has brought no real change in the similes. They are still the same two aspects of nature: animal and thing.

As Achaeans and Trojans are now equal in the eyes of Homer, the simile shifts to their weapons. The stones they hurl against one another are like the snowflakes that cover, indifferently, the fertile earth.[12] We are at war and so in the dead of winter, when nothing grows, but a blanket of snow hides every aspect of life. We are reminded now that the world of war and the world of peace do not jibe; that the winter of war has no sequel like the winter of nature; and that no spring will come after the death of heroes.

Asius frets at the sudden check, which the Lapiths have given, to his high expectations. He compares them to bees or wasps which stand in the way of hunters intent on bigger game.[13] To Homer, Leonteus and Polypoetes are the hunters, but to Asius, naturally, the advance is all on his side. He does not

7. *Iliad* 12. 40–50.
8. Cf. *BT* Scholiast 13. 39, 137.
9. Cf. *Iliad* 6. 407.
10. *Iliad* 12. 131–136.
11. *Ibid.* 12. 146–152.
12. *Ibid.* 12. 156–160.
13. *Ibid.* 12. 167–172 (cf. BT Scholiast). So O. Becker interprets it: *Das Bild des Weges,* pp. 44–45 *(Hermes Einzelschrift.* Heft 4, 1937).

acknowledge the reversal but thinks of them as a slight bother in his way. Thus again as Asius drew an image from animate, so Homer drew his from inanimate nature: snow and bees continue the comparison of animal and thing. Even Zeus follows Homer's lead, sending first an eagle and then a whirlwind as omens:[14] but whereas Homer gives us images, Zeus gives the heroes the things themselves. Omens spell out before their eyes what Homer's similes spell out for us.

After Zeus has shown his presence, Homer adapts his simile of snowflakes to this divine interference. Zeus now makes it snow, and the earth no longer seems a simple entity: Homer picks out mountain-tops, plains steep headlands, and the worked fields of men.[15] With the entrance of Zeus, civil man also enters: he becomes part of the landscape. Men have been so far only huntsmen; now they are farmers as well.

Zeus rouses Sarpedon his son, who charges like a lion among cows or sheep.[16] Men are now cowherds and shepherds. The peaceful world fills out. As the war itself is elaborated, more and more elements are seen in its mirror. Every aspect of war refracts an aspect of peace. The heroes are shadowed, in whatever they do, by the world they left behind. But Sarpedon not only is lion-like, he also is, with Glaucus, a black hurricane.[17] Never can the heroes escape from being both animal and thing.

Achaeans and Trojans have exhausted the animal world. Their counterparts exist now only among men. They fight like two men squabbling over a boundary.[18] War becomes a conventional dispute, that no longer is similar to the natural conflict between lion and sheep.[19] It is man-made and arbitrary, without a true reflection in nature. The similes become more petty. After being like wind and lions, they seem to be like a woman who weighs out wool barely sufficient for her children.[20] For her wool she receives a wage, even as eternal fame is the reward for the Achaeans and Trojans, that they will hand down to their children. But her wage is mean and unseemly, while they think fame glorious. They deceive themselves, she is an honest woman: *gynê chernêtis alêthês*. Seen by the eyes of peace, their war is foolish and of little worth.

Hector raises a stone against the Achaean gate, carrying it as easily as a shepherd carries fleece.[21] His stone is as light as wool, and he himself but a shepherd. Neither the purpose of the war, nor the heroes themselves find any

14. *Ibid.* 12. 200–207, 252–255.
15. *Ibid.* 12. 278–289; cf. 5. 557.
16. *Ibid.* 12. 293, 299–308.
17. *Ibid.* 12. 375–376.
18. *Ibid.* 12. 421–424.
19. Cf. *Iliad* 22. 261–264.
20. *Iliad* 12. 433–436.
21. *Ibid.* 12. 451–455.

glory in peace. If we wish to be impressed by them, we must keep our eye on inanimate nature. So Hector is likened to swift-coming night, and on this note of dead nature the book ends.[22]

We have followed the hero through a series of similes, which shifted back and forth between animal and thing; but this alternation was not simply repetitive: for it emphasized always more openly, in each successive image, how little adapted the hero was to peace; how only wind, snow, and night really suited him; and how little in common have men and human beings. Man at war is half thing and half beast, but there is no nobility, no greatness in him, if we think on peace. Homer does not glorify war. As we become involved in the destinies of his heroes, he whispers more and more insistently, "there is a world elsewhere."

In the thirteenth book the similes are more concerned with the battle itself than with the heroes; and as neither side overwhelms the other, the similes reflect this stalemate, animating the inanimate and stilling the force and motion in animals. Thus it is built on a series of paradoxical images. The Trojans, massed like fire or a whirlwind, advance behind Hector: the fire contains all of their flashy persistence (most evident in Hector), while the wind is their inevitable march, whose bluster belongs less to Hector than to his troops.[23] Hector himself is then compared to a boulder, that, breaking loose from a crag, rolls until it comes to the plain, where it can proceed no farther "however much it desires."[24] A thing is granted life unnaturally, until its course is finally checked and it is brought back to its natural state; while in the death of Imbrius, who falls like an ash cut down by an axe, the reverse takes place: what should naturally stand upright is laid low, and its "delicate foliage," that once was held high on a conspicuous mountain, draws near the earth.[25] And again, once Imbrius lies upon the ground, the two Ajax raise him up, like lions which grasp in their jaws a goat.[26]

Idomeneus returns to his tent and puts on his armor: he resembles a lightning-flash sent by Zeus but, unlike his image he runs back to the war.[27] The steady streak of his brilliance has been set in motion, and thus preserves the double aspect of motion and rest with which the book started. His companion Meriones is compared to "swift Ares," while both together are like Ares and Phobos, who arm now the Ephyroi, now the Phlegyae: so impetus is united with impartiality, their loyalty to the Achaeans with their indifference (as war-

22. *Ibid.* 12. 463.
23. *Ibid.* 13. 39, 53.
24. *Ibid.* 13. 137–142.
25. *Ibid.* 13. 178–181.
26. *Ibid.* 13. 198–202.
27. *Ibid.* 13. 242–245.

riors) to either side.[28] And having decided where they should lend their aid, Meriones again is compared to "swift Ares" and Idomeneus to fire.[29]

The battle itself is next likened to the rush of shrill winds that raise a great cloud of dust, which in turn hovers over the earth.[30] Achaeans and Trojans are brought to a stillstand, their opposed desires endeavoring to move (like the boulder of Hector), but their equality resulting in a stationary cloud (like the level plain that stopped Hector).

Asius comes up to protect the corpse of Othoneus, and he is cut down like an oak or a white poplar or a tall pine.[31] Asius dies like Imbrius, and what is naturally erect carpenters will fashion into a ship. Idomeneus attacks Alcathous, whom, although he wishes to flee, Poseidon charms to the spot; and he stands as rigidly as a tree or a stele.[32] Thus he who wished to stand falls, and he who wished to move remains. War has inverted the world of nature and of men.

Aeneas advances against Idomeneus, who, instead of flight, only thinks of holding his ground, and now, when the image of a tree would be appropriate,[33] Homer likens him to a boar, that bristles its back at the approach of men, its eyes flashing fire in defiance.[34] What should be permanent changes, and what should be in motion holds fast. Aeneas, on the other hand, is like a ram who waits for the sheep to follow him.[35] He retains the stationary fire of Hector, while his men continue the first image of the wind. So when he and Idomeneus stand before one another, they seem like Ares, as if their conflict has been cancelled, and they are found together in a single image.

Meriones returns to prominence as "swift Ares," even though Achaeans and Trojans are drawn closely together about the dead Ascalaphus; but he soon becomes a vulture, as he snatches the spear he cast and falls back among his troops.[36]

Adamas attacks Antilochus and, though he launches his spear with energy, it fails to penetrate the shield but remains there like a burnt stake: Poseidon has checked it and deprived it of its strength.[37] As Adamas retreats Meriones hits him, and, like an unwilling ox bound by ropes, he struggles gaspingly but

---

28. *Ibid.* 13. 295–303.
29. *Ibid.* 13. 328, 330.
30. *Ibid.* 13. 334–338.
31. *Ibid.* 13. 389–391.
32. *Ibid.* 13. 434–438.
33. Cf. *Iliad* 12. 132–136, 146–150.
34. *Iliad* 13. 471–475.
35. *Ibid.* 13. 487–495.
36. *Ibid.* 13. 526–533.
37. *Ibid.* 13. 560–565.

in vain.[38] His forceful spear becomes a lifeless stake and he himself a bound ox: the purposes both of weapon and of man have vanished.

Helenus shoots an arrow at Menelaus, but his breastplate deflects it, as if it were a winnowing-fan, from which beans or peas bounce off in a light wind.[39] All the force in the arrow is transferred into a harmless pea, while the solid breastplate becomes a moving fan. Again the reality has been reversed in the simile.

Meriones kills Harpalion, who lies stretched upon the earth like a worm.[40] Just as the arrow of Helenus lost its swiftness in a contemptible simile, so Harpalion loses all his dignity as the poor worm. The heroic world has almost stopped.

Achaeans and Trojans fight like blazing fire, and the Achaeans try to push back flamelike Hector.[41] Though a mass of fire, Hector moves, and all the motion of the Achaeans is spent in vain. The two Ajax stand by one another like two yoked oxen, who with a single spirit drag the plow: but unlike the simile they do not move.[42] Thus Hector like fire advances and the Ajax like oxen stand firm.

What has been up to now a concealed paradox at last is revealed in Hector's penultimate simile: he charges like a snow-covered mountain.[43] No amount of ingenuity can explain that away; but if the sequence of similes is followed, it fits the tenor of the whole book. The correspondence between animate nature and the hero has long broken down, and now not even the inanimate world can be twisted to suit him. The Trojans fight like savage winds and stir up the sea, and as crest of wave follows wave, so they move in a perpetual order, though they effect no breech in the Achaean ranks;[44] and Hector is at last compared to "mortal-destroying Ares," who, though he tries everywhere, cannot make the enemy yield.[45]

In the twelfth book the heroes were alternately animal and thing; in the thirteenth they acquire a new dimension – they sometimes are compared to gods.[46] The reason for this is obvious: Poseidon has disguised himself as a man and is present among them.[47] Once the gods actively interfere, the merely natural world no longer suffices as a source for Homer's imagery. He must

38. *Ibid.* 13. 570–575.
39. *Ibid.* 13. 588–592.
40. *Ibid.* 13. 653–655.
41. *Ibid.* 13. 673. 687–688.
42. *Ibid.* 13. 703–708.
43. *Ibid.* 13. 754–755.
44. *Ibid.* 13. 795–801.
45. *Ibid.* 13. 802–808.
46. Cf. *Iliad* 12. 130, 188.
47. Cf. *Iliad* 12. 465–466.

transcend the bounds of everyday life and compare the heroes not to what we see and know, but to that which is beyond our knowledge. The heroes at first were made familiar to us, but now only the supernatural can make intelligible their superhuman virtues. As they take on the semblance of what is above them, they become more remote and retreat farther away from us; and such a transformation entails a kind of perversion of the once-natural world. All the motion in the hero and his arms is brought to a halt, even as their fixity is set in motion: a tall pine falls, a wild boar stands still. Thus Homer, in elevating the heroes to a divine status, has been forced to alienate them from nature.

Chapter X
Achilles' and Hector's Similes

Heroes are not given much to poetry: they rarely see their enemies as anything other than men to be killed. They leave to Homer the beautifying of their world.[1] Asius likens the Lapiths to wasps or bees, because his disappointment is so great at being thwarted; he is irritated and chagrined by the insignificance of the enemy.[2] So when Menelaus described Hector metaphorically – "he has the terrible force of fire" – we can imagine how frightened he feels.[3] But that was only a prelude to Hector's own image for Achilles: "I shall go against him, even if his hands are like fire, if his hands are like fire, and his force burning iron."[4] In the very repetition of the phrase we can feel the power of Achilles: he is something unquenchable. That Achilles, to be adequately conceived of, demands a simile, is the greatest tribute Hector could pay him; but that Hector summons up such a description only to dismiss it, gives us an index as well to his own greatness.

Although Achilles and Hector are often compared to animals– eagles, hawks, lions and dogs – their largest group of similes concerns fire. Fire is unlike all other elements, for it contains within itself its own destruction: as it burns it is consumed, and it dies with the end of its opponent. It is an exact image for wrath.

Sometimes Hector's (or Achilles') armor is likened to fire,[5] but more often they themselves are fire, which flashes from their eyes.[6] And this fury lives not just in their faces, but even more in their work: "As portentous fire rages through deep mountain-glens, and the forests, thickly-set and flourishing on the mountain, are burnt, and the wind charging everywhere fans the flame, so Achilles, armed with his sword, rushed everywhere like a god."[7] Achilles as fire seems equal to a god; and Hector might equally be either Ares

---

1. The poetic gifts of Achilles are by no means common; cf. *Iliad* 1. 225; 9. 189, 323–325; 16. 7–11; 21. 280–283; 22. 261–265.
2. *Iliad* 12. 167–172.
3. *Ibid.* 17. 565.
4. *Ibid.* 20. 371–372.
5. *Ibid.* 11. 65–66; 22. 134–135; 19. 373–382; cf. 22. 317–319.
6. *Ibid.* 15. 605–610; 19. 16–17, 365–366.
7. *Ibid.* 20. 490–493; cf. 13. 53. 688; 17. 88–89; 18. 154; 20. 423; 21. 12–16.

or fire.[8] But Homer has another name for fire besides *pyr* or *phlox:* Hephaestus is not only his divine blacksmith, who made Agamemnon's sceptre and Achilles' armor, but he uses his name for fire itself.[9] Hephaestus both makes and destroys: the heroes burn with his fire as they wield his weapons. Their armor and their persons show the dual aspect of Hephaestus. To be his work and to work with his fire would seem the aim of heroic ambition. He is their all.

Although Hector numerically rivals Achilles in similes of fire, he cannot claim "he is pure air and fire, and the dull elements of earth and water never appear in him." He is in fact often like a storm, or a river, or the sea, to all of which Achilles is never compared.[10] He has more bluster in his nature than Achilles; his energies are more widely scattered. He is not as concentrated in his person, nor does he plunge as headlong toward his fate. His violence rages on the surface; he is not everywhere pure flame. He has other sentiments than fury. He is "watered-down."

Achilles has a fear of drowning. The thought that he might be crowned by the Xanthus, like a young swineherd whom a winter torrent sweeps away, provokes his bitterest complaints against his mother Thetis.[11] As fire and light, fanned by his ambition, he trembles before all obscurity. To be quenched, as it were, and returned to "earth and water" is the most shameful doom: deprived of all distinction and confounded with a swineherd.[12] Achilles ridicules the lineage of Asteropaeus, whose ancestor was the river Axius: "As Zeus is stronger than rivers that flow into the sea, so the generation of Zeus is stronger than that of a river . . . nothing can fight against Zeus the son of Cronus, not even the strong Achelous is his equal, from whence all rivers and every sea and all fountains and springs arise: but even he fears the lightning and terrible thunder of great Zeus, whenever he makes it crash in the heavens."[13] Zeus the hurler of lightning and thunder is greater than water: Achilles boasts his descent from fire and forgets that his own mother is a sea-goddess.[14] If he is more closely related to the gods on his mother's side, Achilles prefers to emphasize the divine lineage of his father: for there is something womanish and humane about Thetis that does not fit in with Achilles' image of himself.

When Zeus makes the gods take sides, the river Xanthus is pitted against

8. *Ibid.* 15. 605; cf. 13. 53–54.
9. *Ibid.* 2. 426; 9. 468; 17. 88; 23. 33.
10. Storm: *Iliad* 11. 297, 305; 12. 40; river: 5. 597–599; waves: 11. 307; 15. 624.
11. *Iliad* 21. 273–283.
12. Cf. *Iliad* 7. 99–100; Tacitus *Annales* i. 70. 1–3.
13. *Iliad* 21. 190–199; cf. 124–132; 20. 390–392; 14. 244–246. 21. 195 is interpolated; cf. G. Bolling, *External Evidence,* pp. 188–189; Pasquali, G., *Storia della Tradizione,* pp. 225–227. Note that Achilles does not know the power of Oceanus: only the gods and Homer know.
14. Cf. *Iliad* 20. 104–107.

Hephaestus.[15] Water defends the Trojans, fire Achilles: and fire triumphs. As Achilles surpasses Asteropaeus in ancestry (as fire does water), so Hephaestus destroys Xanthus. It is the triumph of art over nature.

15. *Iliad* 20. 73–74.

Chapter XI
Heroic Ambition

Hector is bold enough to declare the ultimate end of his ambition; he would assign to himself all the prerogatives of the gods: "Would that I might be in this way honored as Athena and Apollo are honored, as surely as this day brings evil to the Argives."[1] Hector does not contrast the impossibility of his wish with the certainty of his success, but rather his success colors his desire. Victory is so certain, it is so much a foregone conclusion, that he presents the impossible as something tangible and real. "My concern," he says to the Trojans, "is not for the outcome of tomorrow's battle – that is as good as ours – but for my immortality." His ambition overleaps the present and reaches out beyond the immediate. Even if to become immortal is unlikely, to be honored like Apollo and Athena is not; so that, as his certainty about the morrow gives him assurance of divine honors, these honors in turn strengthen his hope for immortality.

Since Hector will win on the morrow, he deserves to be honored like Athena and Apollo. He picks the foremost gods on each side: he does not wish partisan honor but true honor, based on something that even the enemy's gods must acknowledge.[2] His excellence would force their admiration. So Homer, when he wishes to praise the excellence of the Achaeans' battle-order, invokes Ares as well as Athena;[3] and not just because they are the gods of battle,[4] for when the battle is fiercest over Patroclus' corpse, "neither Ares nor Athena, beholding it, blame their fighting, not even if wrath came into them."[5] If the gods were angry, they could not find fault: no passion, which might warp their judgment, could diminish their praise.

Hector wants to be immortal and ageless: it is his final goal. The end of his action, to destroy the Achaeans, should issue in the perfection of his being, immortality. But he wants even more: "Would that I might be the son of aegis-bearing Zeus, and would that awesome Hera had borne me."[6] To be the son of

1. *Iliad* 8. 538–541.
2. Cf. *Iliad* 2. 371–372; 4. 288–289; *Odyssey* 11. 543–547.
3. *Iliad* 13. 126–128.
4. *Ibid.* 18. 516.
5. *Ibid.* 17. 397–399; cf. 20. 358–359.
6. *Ibid.* 13. 825–826.

Zeus and of Hera is his ambition: to be in fact what Homer grants him in simile pushes him on. If he could break through the simile, and become what he resembles, if he could change "like to a mortal-destroying Ares" to Ares himself, he would be satisfied. According to Poseidon he believes that he is.[7] To affirm, to boast, to pray (they are the same verb *euchesthai)* means the same thing to Hector. Both in the past of his lineage and in the future of his desire stand the gods. If he could return to his origins, he would achieve his end. In the inability of Hector and Achilles to come full circle lies their tragedy.

We must not think that Achilles and Hector are alone in this wish: even lesser heroes are compared to a divinity or honored by their people like a god. But Hector is not content with the praise of his own fellow citizens: he wants all men, any man, to praise him.[8] Universal praise, which does not perish, is the closest he can approach to immortality. Fame is its substitute. If Sarpedon were fated to be immortal and ageless, he would not stay in battle; but as he cannot remain alive forever, he must nobly act and die, so that he may stay alive in the memory of others.[9]

The love of fame animates not only the hero but also his horse, and if we just glance at how the classics described and exploited the horse, we can see more readily why Homer bound them together, and gave to Achilles immortal horses.

> And Achilles' horse
> Makes many Thetis' sons.[10]

The horse, of all animals, is the most naturally ambitious. It has *thymos* ("spiritedness"), matching man in this as in almost all other things.[11] Xenophon speaks as if in his time *thymos* was the proper name for a horse's spirit and *orgê* for a man's; Parmenides likens his own desire to mares;

7 *Ibid.* 13. 54, 802; cf. 7. 298; 14. 386–391; 24. 258–259.

8. *Ibid.* 7. 87–91.

9. *Ibid.* 12. 322–328.

10. *Ibid.* 16. 154; 23. 277.

11. *Thymos* of a horse: *Iliad* 8, 189; 10. 492, 531; 11. 520; 16. 382, 469; 23. 468. Neither the horse nor any other animal has *phrenes;* for the difference between them, cf. 2. 371–372 with 4. 288–289; 13. 493–494. The phrase *kata phrena kai kata thymon* usually expresses indecision: the hero is inclined one way by *thymos,* another way by *phrên:* it is not tautological (1. 193; 11. 411; 17. 106; 18. 15; cf. 10. 507). Homer seems to distinguish between singular *phrên* and plural *phrenes:* the singular is never used in a bad sense, but often of pleasure, rarely of grief; the plural is often in a bad sense, rarely of pleasure, often of grief and other violent passions. "Pure" passions are entitled to the singular, "impure" to the plural; the pure ones seem to be fear for others and pleasure for oneself (of fear: 1. 555; 9. 244; 10. 538; of pleasure: 6. 285; 8. 559; 9. 186 (cf. 184), *passim).* Zeus' undivided will is singular (2. 3; 10. 45–46; 12. 173; 19. 125; 20. 23), but it becomes plural when perturbed and divided (8. 360, 446; 13. 631; 14, 165, 294; 16. 435,

Socrates compares the good appetites of the soul to a noble horse: "upright, well-knit, high-arched neck, aquiline nose, white, black eyes, a lover of honor;"[12] and as the horse is the most erotic of creatures after man (his eros is both sexual and ambitious),[13] Vergil in the third *Georgic,* as part of his theme, shifts from the warhorse to love and from love to the love of glory,

Tantus amor laudem, tantae est victoria curae.[14]
(. . . so great is their love of praise, victory is so great a care.)

When Dolon offers to spy on the Achaeans, he makes Hector swear to give him, on the condition of his success, the chariot and the horses of Achilles.[15] He can think of no greater glory than that: they are at the height of his ambition. To possess Achilles' immortal horses is to become almost immortal oneself; for as they would be forever, they would always keep flourishing one's fame. They would be a more lasting monument than a grave, that may either be mistaken for something else or completely washed away.[16] They are, however, beyond Dolon's capacities, and not even Hector could manage them.[17]

Nothing indicates more exactly the difference between the *Iliad* and the *Odyssey* than Achilles' horses and Odysseus' dog.[18] The horses weep for Patroclus but will outlast Achilles and all men; while Argus, who was beautiful and swift, dies at the sight of Odysseus.[19] His life is so closely bound up with his master's that he cannot live well without him: but Achilles' horses will continue to be both beautiful and swift forever. Their immortality prevents their affection from ever being serious;[20] they do not really belong to any man, nor are they ever domesticated. They stand even beyond Achilles, and represent the futility of his end.

Achilles' horses, having all the qualities desired in a horse, mixed, so to speak, with no corruptible matter, are quite naturally divine. Immortality and agelessness seem to be the reward for their virtue; and if man's perfection were the same as a horse's, then Achilles, who equals them in swiftness as in

444; 19. 121. 127). Consider the beautiful uses of *phrên* in the *Odyssey* (6. 147; 19. 471), the only instances, I believe, of the singular used of anger and of grief.
12. Xenophon *de re equestri* ix. 2; Parmenides fr. 1, 1; Plato *Phaedrus* 253d3–253e1; cf. *Iliad* 10. 436–437.
13. Aristotle *HA* 575b31–33, cf. 604b25–27; Vergil *Georgica* iii. 266; Shakespeare *Henry V* 3. 7. 1–88; *Venus and Adonis* 259–324,385–396.
14. *Georgica* iii. 112.
15. *Iliad* 10. 322–323. cf. 305–306.
16. Cf. *Iliad* 7. 86–91, 446–451; 12. 13–33, 326–333.
17. *Iliad* 10. 401–404; 17. 75–78.
18. Cf. Geddes, *The Problem of the Homeric Poems,* pp. 205–235.
19. *Odyssey* 17, 291–323.
20. Cf. *Iliad* 1. 573–574; 15. 138–141; 21. 379–380.

beauty, would be a god. That his virtues do not secure for him immortality points to the only flaw in his nature.

When Achilles has cut through Hector's throat, Hector is still able to speak.[21] Homer makes it almost grotesquely clear; for Achilles' javelin seems to have gone out of its way to allow Hector speech: "The bronze-heavy javelin did not sever his wind-pipe, so that he might tell him something and reply in words." It is Hector's very act of speaking, not so much what he says, that should instruct Achilles. Man is an animal that speaks even on the verge of death, while Achilles' horses, perfect though they are, can only speak when Hera has given them voice.[22] The will of a god makes them the spokesmen of Achilles' fate: but Hector needs no divine aid to foretell, even more precisely, Achilles' death.[23] The horse is the measure of man's humanity. For not to Achilles, who is all action, but to Odysseus, whose speech is like the winter's snow, is immortality offered.[24] Calypso promises to make Odysseus immortal and ageless; but he refuses on the very grounds which Achilles would have given for acceptance.

When Odysseus walks through the palace of Alcinous, he sees bronze walls, gold doors, silver jambs, and last, "gold and silver hounds were on each side, which Hephaestus had cleverly made to be the guardians of great-hearted Alcinous' palace, immortal and ageless forever."[25] Here is what Calypso had promised: here is what Odysseus rejected. To be like a golden hound, a work of art, a thing forged on the anvil of Hephaestus, is immortality. Why Odysseus prefers Penelope to Calypso, toil and trouble to heart-ease, his own rocky kingdom to a kind of paradise, the golden hounds of Hephaestus explain. He prefers to remain mortal and human: to be a person and not a thing.

21. *Iliad* 22. 328–329.
22. *Ibid.* 19. 407.
23. *Ibid.* 19. 416–417; 22. 358–360; cf. Xenophon *de re equestri* viii. 13.
24. *Odyssey* 5. 136; 7. 257; 23. 336; *Iliad* 18. 105–106; 19. 217–219; 3. 216–224; cf. 15. 741; 16. 630–631.
25. *Odyssey* 7. 91–94.

Part II
Plot

Introduction

It is very difficult at the present time to talk sensibly about the Homeric hero, for not only has "virtue" itself become an anachronism, we ourselves no longer responding to it at once, but also, because of this unawareness, we either dismiss with contempt the tragic hero, who embodies all virtues, or we rank him beyond his worth. We have lost a just appreciation of virtue, which only the world around us, and not poetry alone, can supply. Unlike the philosopher, who may write down all of his thoughts, the tragic hero resists translation. No matter how well he is described, unless we have seen him beforehand in action, and know what kind of man he is, the poetic hero will ever remain alien to us. Unless we are in immediate sympathy with Achilles, and regard not his submission but his apostasy as the sign of his greatness, the *Iliad* will never seem real. His submission, which his humanity imposes upon him, signifies his tragedy: but his greatness lies in his disregard of all civility. We, however, tend to turn his virtue into a vice, repelled by his superhuman excellence and secretly pleased with his downfall; or if we are more unconventional, we will blame "society" for his own failure and assign his defects to his opponents. The reason why we are so apt to distort the tragic hero, ignoring either his vices or his virtues, is the absence of examples in our midst, by whom we could be guided in our estimate of their poetic counterparts. Indeed the "Homeric Problem" perhaps could hardly have arisen, had not the hero as a reality no longer been recognized and understood. Most other ages have had an Alcibiades or a Marlborough to lend substance to the poet's fiction; so that the paradoxical mean between virtue and vice which the tragic hero maintains, being both better than ourselves and yet unexceptional in justice and virtue, was at once convincing. If we, however, must look in vain for contemporary examples of the hero, our only recourse is to fictional accounts that may impress more deeply than the *Iliad* itself. Where then are we to find them? Plutarch's *Lives* perhaps would have served us best; but if his "moralizing historiography," which was "for centuries the mental fare of the reading public," was "weighed by the nineteenth century and found wanting,"[1] we cannot hope that a reference to him now would suffice to restore him and make intelligible to us the tragic hero. Although Plutarch has no other

---

1. W. Den Boer, *Laconian Studies*, Preface.

theme than the hero – and how difficult it is either to praise or blame him[2] – he is too old-fashioned to be of any use. We need a poet whom we still read and partly understand; so I have invoked the aid of Shakespeare's *Coriolanus,* not in order to compare it with the *Iliad* and note the differences, but rather to appeal to everyone's imagination, which *Coriolanus*, stripped of divine intervention, might more easily excite. Since it is much shorter than the *Iliad* (as well as simpler), its actors are forced to be more out-spoken than Achilles and Hector, who only hint at what Coriolanus and Aufidius state openly. By glossing the *Iliad* with this play, and thus making it less inaccessible and more pertinent, I hope that my analysis of the *Iliad* proper may carry more conviction than it otherwise might have done.

The play's motif is the transformation of Coriolanus from a man to a god: it is, like the *Iliad,* an experiment in immortality. Coriolanus' progressive alienation from Rome, from his friends, from his family mark his progress toward a divine status. He becomes at last alienated from his own body and ends up as a mere thing. He is thought at first to be a god by others: he becomes a god at the end in his own opinion. The play moves, as it were, from simile to fact, from metaphor to tragedy.

Caius Marcius, outraged by the people's insistence on their rights, who are in war nothing but "cushions, leaden spoons, irons of a doit," comes on the scene, after Menenius has likened them to a body's limbs and the Senate to its belly, crying[3]

> What's the matter, you dissentious rogues, That, rubbing the poor
> itch of your opinion Make yourselves scabs?

The people are to him superfluous sores, whose authority (vested in their tribunes) he cannot respect, for they lack all power. Menenius had given them a place, however small, in the commonwealth; Marcius denies them all place, except what they might unlawfully usurp. They are worse than strangers: they are a hostile infection. Their weakness constantly increases his contempt, which reaches its first climax in the battle where his own prowess earns him the title "Coriolanus."[4] So even while he curses the people as enemies, he is assuming the name of the enemy's city. In his Roman triumph, he becomes less Roman.

When Lartius hears how Marcius entered the gates of Corioli alone, he announces the first stage in his becoming more than human:[5]

O noble fellow!

2. Cf., e.g., *Cimon* II.
3. *Coriolanus* 1.1.163465 (following the lineation of the Cambridge *Works of Shakespeare,* John Dover Wilson, ed.).
4. *Ibid.* 1. 9. 62–66.
5. *Ibid.* 1. 4. 53–55.

> Who sensibly outdares his senseless sword,
> And when it bows, stand'st up!

He is like "his sword, death's stamp,"[6]

> Where it did mark, it took; from face to foot
> He was a thing of blood, whose every motion
> Was timed with dying cries.

Once set in motion, he cannot stop but seems a perpetual instrument of death, indifferent to the object of his slaughter and unsparing of himself. The operations of his sword have been communicated to himself; and, now that he is transmuted into that which he himself should wield, whoever has, can use him.[7] He becomes like the spoil he so much had despised.

But Coriolanus needs an enemy, no matter who it may be; for what Valeria says of his son applies equally well to himself:[8]

> I saw him run after a gilded butterfly; and when he caught it, he
> let it go again; and after it again; and over and over he comes, and
> up again; catched it again; or whether his fall enraged him, or how
> 'twas, he did so set his teeth, and tear it; I warrant, how he mam-
> mocked it!"

Coriolanus thinks all things are gilded butterflies, whose brilliance irritates his ambition, but whose capture deprives them of their worth. To attain or lose his object is equally fatal; his restlessness longs for ever-greater aggrandizement. Surfeit would kill him.

The envious tribunes, Sicinius and Brutus, are the first to notice his god-like state:[9]

> As if that whatsoever god who leads him
> Was slily crept into his human powers, And gave him graceful
> posture.

And when Coriolanus grows angry, calling the plebs "those measles," Brutus remarks:[10]

> You speak of the people,
> As if you were a god to punish; not A man of their infirmity.

To him Sicinius was a "rotten thing," but to Brutus he is the "disease that must be cut away;" and though Menenius objects to the Tribunes' remedy, yet he

6. *Ibid.* 2. 2. 105–108; cf. 5. 4. 18–22.
7. *Ibid.* 2. 2. 108–127.
8. *Ibid.* 1. 3. 61–66, cf. 67.
9. *Ibid.* 2. 1. 216–218, cf. 262–263.
10. *Ibid.* 3. 1. 80–82, cf. 254–259.

thinks Coriolanus is "a limb that has but a disease," or a "foot gangrened."[11] Not only the tribunes but Menenius, who before had called the people limbs, must now call Coriolanus so. He and the people reverse their roles: he becomes the boils and plagues he thought they were.[12] From being at the center of the body politic, he is now an infection at its extremity. "Too absolute" and "too noble for this world," hating all dissemblance and rhetoric, he can only play what he is;[13] and unable to be a traitor to himself, he prefers to be a traitor to Rome. He is decreed an outcast. "I shall be loved when I am lack'd," he tells his mother, as if in echo of Achilles' threat:[14] but Achilles did not have to help the Trojans in his own person – Zeus was his surrogate – while Coriolanus enters into open conspiracy with Aufidius, the enemy whom he had most hated and most admired.[15] As his hatred of the people had turned him, metaphorically, into one of those whom he thought most inimical, so now his former hatred of Aufidius seals his alliance.[16] Aufidius welcomes him, compares him to Jupiter, proclaims him a "noble thing" and "Mars."[17] He assumes all the aspects of an avenging deity.

The Volscians make their attack on Roman territory; and Cominius brings the news that Coriolanus has joined them:[18]

> He is their god; he leads them like a thing
> Made by some other deity than Nature,
> That shapes man better; and they follow him
> Against us brats with no less confidence
> Than boys pursuing summer butterflies, or butchers killing flies.

The gilded butterfly that his son had chased, as if in sympathy with his own attack upon the Volscians, is transformed, by his wrath's alchemy, into Rome and her people. Though his opponent is different, his fury is the same. Cominius beseeches him, who "wants nothing of a god but eternity and a heaven to throne in,"[19] to spare his native city, urging an "old acquaintance," but[20]

> 'Coriolanus'
> He would not answer to; forbad all names;

11. *Ibid.* 3. 1. 178, 219–221, 293–295, 304–306, cf. 234–235, 308–309.
12. *Ibid.* 1. 4. 30–34.
13. *Ibid.* 3. 1. 254–259; 3. 2. 14–16, 39–41, 46–64, 99–123; cf. 4. 5. 139; 5. 3. 40–42.
14. *Iliad.* 4. 1. 15; cf. 4. 6. 42–46; *Il.* 1. 240–244; 9. 351–355.
15. *Coriolanus* 1. 1. 229–231; cf. 1. 10. 4–16.
16. Cf. *ibid.* 2. 2. 15–22; 4. 4. 12–26.
17. *Ibid.* 4. 5. 104–121, cf. 197–198.
18. *Ibid.* 4. 6. 91–96; cf. 5. 4. 11–14; *King Lear* 4. 1. 36–37.
19. *Coriolanus.* 5. 4. 23–24.
20. *Ibid.* 5. 1. 10–15.

> He was a kind of nothing, titleless,
> Till he had forged himself a name i' th' fire
> Of burning Rome.

Having dropped the surname Coriolanus, which had been in his exile the one thing that remained his,[21] he wishes now to be known as "Romanus": he has switched sides, but stayed, ironically, the same.

Unmoved by Cominius and later by Menenius, his mother, wife and son come to petition him, when the Romans send them as a last resort; but he resolves to refuse them:[22]

> I'll never
> Be such a gosling to obey instinct, but stand
> As if a man were author of himself
> And knew no other kin.

Only for a moment, however, does he succeed in checking instinct; for he soon succumbs to natural affection. But having failed to acquire "Romanus" as a title, and Aufidius having denied his right to the "stolen name Coriolanus, in Corioli," he belongs nowhere.[23] Traitor to Rome, he seems to have betrayed his adopted city. His divinity played him false; it admitted of no political sanctions; it passed beyond his own power: he became its slave. He could not fulfill the obligations that the image of himself, made by others and perfected by himself, imposed on him. Out of place everywhere, an alien deity in the shape of a man, his nature trips him up in the end. Once having gone beyond the bounds that he thought conventional, he could not return to convention.[24] The no-man's land, into which he had trespassed "like to a lonely dragon,"[25] was set with the lures of his own conceits, that drew him finally to his ruin.

Achilles is Coriolanus: both are gods in their wrath. Achilles' attack on Agamemnon's authority corresponds to Coriolanus' refusal to acknowledge the tribune's office; his loss of Briseis to the loss of the consulate; the ingratitude of Agamemnon to that of the people; his withdrawal from the battle to the other's banishment; the fulfillment of his wish that Zeus avenge his wrongs to Coriolanus' invasion of Rome; his rejection of the embassy of Ajax and Odysseus to the other's denial of Cominius and Menenius; and his acceptance of his duty, after Patroclus' death, corresponds to Coriolanus' sparing of Rome after his family's petition. But that Patroclus had to die before Achilles returns to the war, that Patroclus is not even related to him, that his mother is divine and his father far away, and that he is not married: all this deepens

21. *Ibid.* 4. 5. 76.
22. *Ibid.* 5. 3. 34–37; cf. 149–153.
23. *Ibid.* 5. 6. 85–101.
24. Cf. *ibid.* 2. 3. 116–120.
25. *Ibid.* 4. 1. 30; cf. 4. 7. 23; 5. 4. 12–14.

Achilles' tragedy. His ties to this world are more attenuated than Coriolanus';
and as it is easier for him to break them, so it is harder to renew them. Drained
of all human substance, isolated from other men, but unable to become divine,
Achilles cracks, turns monstrous, and dies.

Chapter I
The Gods

If the heroes regard divinity as the end of their ambition, we must first see what the gods do – before we can understand why Achilles and Hector, Sarpedon and Ajax, are so desirous to become like them. Blunt Ajax states the paradox of heroic virtue: "Alas, even a fool would know that Zeus himself defends the Trojans: the spears of all, no matter whether good or bad do hurl them, hit their target: Zeus makes all go straight."[1] Zeus' partiality makes it almost impossible to practice virtue. Were Ajax to retreat, he would be blameless.[2] Zeus can render vain and useless the distinction between good and bad, base and brave. What should prove merit – success – may be wholly undeserved. The javelin-cast of Paris, were Zeus to wish it, would go as straight as that of Hector; if the gods had always favored Nireus, he would have equalled Achilles. Were not the providence of the gods inconstant and fitful,[3] they would obscure completely any natural order of excellence; but as it is, they sometimes withdraw and let the heroes run themselves. Then does the world run true; then we can see the heroes for what they are.

After Achilles sets the prizes for the horse-race, and urges the best Achaeans to compete, Homer gives us the order in which they accept the challenge. First Eumelus, who excelled in horsemanship and had the best horses;[4] then Diomedes with the horses of Aeneias; third Menelaus with one horse of his own and one of Agamemnon's; and then Antilochus.[5] Before Homer tells us who came last, Nestor counsels his son on the power of craft. Although Antilochus' horses are swift-footed, they are slower than the three pairs of horses that entered before him, yet faster than Meriones' which are the slowest of all.[6] Meriones is naturally reluctant to compete: only after Nestor, whose praise of craft gives him a chance, has spoken at length can he bring himself to risk his horses in a contest they cannot possibly win.

1. *Iliad* 17.629–632; cf. 13. 222–227; 20. 242–243, 434–437; *Odyssey* 18. 132–135.
2. Cf. *Iliad* 16. 119–122.
3. Cf. *Iliad* 15. 139–141; 16. 446–447.
4. *Iliad* 23. 288–289; 2. 763–767.
5. *Ibid.* 23. 290–304.
6. *Ibid.* 23. 304, 310, 530.

If we look at the race itself, we see that Homer has presented the horse-men in the order in which they should, but do not win.[7] That Eumelus should have been first, although he comes in last, Achilles, Homer, and all the Achaeans acknowledge; and were it not that Achilles wishes to gratify Antilochus, even in his misfortune he would have taken second prize.[8] Had not Apollo and Athena interfered, Diomedes would have either come in first or tied Eumelus:[9] we shall never know which, but in any case he would be sec-ond. Menelaus was due for third place, but the craft of Antilochus upset him; and yet if the course had been longer, he would have outstripped him.[10] Antilochus then should have been fourth, and Meriones, unequal in skill to the others, fifth.[11]

Two things disturb the natural order: art and providence. If Apollo had not wished to help Eumelus, Athena would not have broken his horses' yoke, nor given more strength to Diomedes' horses.[12] The gods made him who was to be first last, and him who was to be second first. And Antilochus' art put him ahead of Menelaus;[13] but human art is not eternally superior; for the natural slowness of his horses would have eventually betrayed him.[14] Thus providence and art stand very close to one another: both change the hierarchy set up by nature and substitute for it an unpredictable order. The superiority of art is short-lived, and given enough time, nature triumphs: whether the gods too are subject to nature remains to be seen.

Homer has also given a third order, the line-up, that the casting of lots determined. Here no one is in his right place except Menelaus: Eumelus is second, Diomedes last, Antilochus first, Meriones fourth.[15] Menelaus, who was third in excellence and third in victory, is also third when mere accident tells his position. Chance mistakes everyone else but Menelaus: mediocrity is all that you can trust it to find out.

The heroes can never be certain, in whatever they do, that they will be successful. They live in constant apprehension that the gods may interfere; who not only may give them strength but deprive them of victory. They often snatch the heroes from death. At the start of Diomedes' exploits, had not Hephaestus saved Idaeus "hiding him in night," he "would not have escaped a black doom;" but he was saved only because Dares, his father, was a priest of

---

7. Cf. the foot race, *Iliad* 23. 754–792.
8. *Iliad* 23. 536–538, 556.
9. *Ibid.* 23. 382–383.
10. *Ibid.* 23. 526–527.
11. *Ibid.* 23. 530–531.
12. *Ibid.* 23. 383–400.
13. *Ibid.* 23. 515.
14. Cf. *Iliad* 23. 344–348.
15. *Iliad* 23. 352–357.

Hephaestus and might have been vexed if his son had died.[16] Diomedes' bold strength, bestowed by Athena, could not overcome the opposition of Hephaestus, who, as the son of Hera, was partial to the Achaeans, but did not dare disappoint his priest, Trojan though he was.[17]

When Athena sees what Hephaestus has done, she fears lest the other gods might save their own favorites; so, confident that the Achaeans will press their advantage, she persuades Ares, her most formidable enemy, to stand aside, with herself, from the battle.[18] Ares complies, and each Achaean king slays a Trojan: Agamemnon slays Odius, Idomencus Phaestus, Menelaus Scamandrius; Meriones slays Phereclus, Meges Pedaeus, and Euryphylus Hypsenor.[19] Among the Trojans who are slain, Scamandrius was taught to hunt by Artemis; Phereclus was the son of Harmonides, who "knew how to make many curious things, for Pallas Athena loved him;" and Hypsenor was the son of Dolopion, who served as priest to the river Scamander. And yet Scamandrius dies as surely as Odius, when they both turn to flee, even though one was Artemis' favorite; and Phereclus meets the same fate as Padaeus, though the one was illegitimate, and the other had a father who was taught by Athena. Neither Artemis, nor the Scamander, nor Athena saved the heroes to whom they were attached; and they are slain along with those who had before been less fortunate and had always lacked divine protection.

As soon as the gods withdraw, everyone indifferently dies: bastard as well as a priest's son, plain coward and a coward whom Artemis loved. "Loathsome darkness" seized Phaestus, whom no god had ever befriended; and "purple death and strong fate closed the eyes" of Hypsenor, whose father was the priest of the Scamander. The death of neither is much adorned: Homer merely states what happened; but later, when the gods reappear, Aeneias kills Crethon and Orsilochus (their ancestor was a river), and they not only die, when "the end of death covers them," but they die beautifully. They are like two lions who, having caught sheep and cattle, are slain at last by men; and they fall like tall pines.[20] Their death appears not only as itself but as something else: doubled in the simile's reflection, it magically loses all its horror, becoming beautiful and almost pleasant. Heroes may die horribly – Homer sometimes is medically precise – yet in his similes of death, employed only if the gods are present, nothing but a noble death, purged of grossness remains. The gods transfigure death, which is, without them unfeigned, but in their presence more poetic.

16. *Ibid.* 5. 9–24
17. Cf. *Iliad* 20. 297–299.
18. *Iliad.* 5. 29–35.
19. *Ibid.* 5. 35–83.
20. *Ibid.* 5. 541–560.

It might be objected to this, that no distinction can be drawn between Homer and the gods; but, although Homer inserts the gods whenever he pleases, he does not treat them as his own machinery, over which he has any control. He accepts them to be as real as the heroes themselves, and to actively belong to the story; while he rarely shows himself to be present. He only tells what happened, not what he himself has made. To us it may seem a pious fiction, but we are forced to accept it. Homer separates himself from his work: he presents neither the narrative nor the speeches nor the similes as his own; and if they follow a pattern, we must understand their proximate causes, before we can refer everything to Homer.

That the gods alone can inspire a simile about death, holds true throughout the *Iliad;* for even the one exception, that I know of, supplies another proof. Patroclus, whom the gods never prompt or encourage, drives his spear through the jaw of Thestor, and grabbing hold of it, drags him over the rim of his chariot, "as when a man, sitting on an overhanging rock, pulls from the sea a sacred fish with hook and line, so he dragged him gaping on the end of his shining spear."[21] The death of Thestor, ghastly in itself, becomes more ghastly in the simile; for no gods are present but only Homer, who, feeling bound to stand beside Patroclus on his one triumphal day, calls to him as if he himself were there.[22] Homer favors Patroclus and follows him everywhere, calling him "horseman Patroclus" and repeating "you answered him this, Patroclus." To no other hero does Homer seem so attached, but since the gods are absent, he can, as it were, only ensure the aptness and not the beauty of a simile.

When Patroclus has killed Thestor and many other Trojans, and Sarpedon rushes against him, Hera persuades Zeus not to save his son, who soon after is killed by Patroclus.[23] Sarpedon, however, unlike Thestor, dies beautifully – like a white poplar, or an oak, or a stately pine – and nobly – like a high-spirited bull whom a lion slays in the herd. Thestor died like a fish without the benefit of the gods; Sarpedon's death was heralded by bloody drops that Zeus poured down. The gods beautify death; they order the ugly chaos of war; they are the gilders of the heroic world.

We have seen the heroes godless in snatches of war: we must now see them thus over a longer period. Athena and Hera return to Olympus at the end of the fifth book, "having stopped baneful Ares from his slaughter of men;" and the sixth book announces the departure of all the gods.[24] Each event will now be unconditioned by the gods: the heroes will act without them and hence will act differently.

21. *Ibid.* 16. 406–410; cf. *Odyssey* 12. 251–255.
22. *Ibid.* 16. 20, 584, 693,744, 754, 787, 812, 843.
23. *Ibid.* 16. 419–491.
24. *Ibid.* 5.906–908, 6.1; 11.401.

Diomedes kills Axylus, who was "a friend to human beings" – *philos d'ên anthrôpoisi* – "but no one of them warded off his mournful death."[25] When the gods are absent, it is sadly fitting that a philanthropist, whose kindness benefited other mortals but not the gods, should die. He does not share in a divine providence. He is alone.

Menelaus captures Adrastus alive, whose horses had entangled his chariot and spilled him on the ground.[26] As an accident puts him at the mercy of anyone who might find him, Menelaus cannot congratulate himself on his own prowess. He owes everything to chance and nothing to himself; and aware of this, he is willing to accept ransom, until Agamemnon comes up and rebukes him for his leniency, urging him to kill all the Trojans, "even a boy still in his mother's womb." Nothing equals the cruelty of Agamemnon's advice or Menelaus' action. Though Agamemnon himself later kills the two sons of Antimachus, who plead for their lives, he at least defends his decision to kill them; and when Achilles rejects Lycaon's supplication, his excuse is his fury which, ever since Patroclus' death, has overtaken him.[27] Here Agamemnon, without offering any excuse, persuades Menelaus to kill Adrastus; and, Homer adds, "saying what he ought, what is just" *(aisima pareipôn)*. Not only Agamemnon has become cruel but Homer as well; for the gods, who before had taken sides, are now nowhere to be seen. Their partiality had made the heroic world moral; they had set limits to right and wrong, however arbitrary they sometimes may seem; their disapproval, which depended on their affections, had guided Homer in his own judgment. When Achilles refuses to save the life of Tros, who wordlessly grasps his knees, Homer tells us his opinion: "He was not a sweet-tempered man nor mild in spirit;" and when Achilles slays twelve Trojans as an offering to Patroclus, he again blames him: "He resolved evil deeds in his heart;" for Homer, knowing that some gods disapprove of Achilles, can echo their opinion.[28] But now that the gods have lost all interest in human affairs, no one tells the heroes what they ought to do, and without the gods they become monsters.

Hector, encouraged by Helenus, charges the Achaeans, who retreat and cease their slaughter: "They thought some one of the immortals had come down from the starry heaven to aid the Trojans."[29] The Achaeans mistake Hector for a god, when no gods are present; they think he has come from the starry heaven when he is a mortal who crawls upon the earth.[30] As heaven and earth, gods and men, have never been so far apart, the heroes confound them.

25. *Ibid.* 6. 11–19.
26. *Ibid.* 6. 37–65 cf. 2. 831–834.
27. *Ibid.* 11. 122–142; 21. 99–106; cf. 21. 95 with 23. 746–747.
28. *Ibid.* 20. 463–469; 23. 175–176.
29. *Ibid.* 6. 108–109.
30. Cf. *Iliad* 6. 108, 123, 128–129, 131, 142, 527.

Diomedes, whom Athena had so recently favored, cannot tell whether Glaucus is a god or a man; he is as uncertain as Odysseus when he confronts Nausicaa.[31] He asks Glaucus: "Who are you, O most mighty power, of mortal human beings *(kata thnêtôn anthrôpôn)?* Only here does a hero call another to his face a "human being" and not a "he-man."[32] Diomedes reckons in absolutes: Glaucus is either human or divine; he cannot be, what he himself once was, divinely inspired.

Critics have been puzzled that Diomedes, who has wounded Aphrodite and Ares, should now be unwilling to fight Glaucus if he turns out to be a god.[33] But there is no difficulty: the gods have departed and left the heroes, Diomedes along with the rest, alone. His ability to distinguish between man and god depended on Athena's favor:[34] as soon as she withdrew from the battle, he knew no more than the Achaeans, to whom Hector seemed a god.

The burden of their mortality oppresses Diomedes and Glaucus. One seems at a loss without the gods, the other sees all men as alike and undistinguishable: "as are the generations of leaves, such are those also of men."[35] Genealogy is a mere succession of men, *akritophyllon*,[36] "undistinguishable leafage." But Glaucus wishes to gloss over his own sense of smallness, and to impress Diomedes with his divine lineage, even if he cannot quite believe it himself. He deals in superlatives: Sisyphus was the *craftiest* of men; Bellerophon said his battle with the Solymi was the *fiercest* he had ever entered; and Bellerophon slew all the men who were *best* in Lycia.[37] Glaucus, the son of Sisyphus, fathered blameless Bellerophon, whose beauty and manliness came from the gods, and whom the gods escorted to Lycia and helped to slay the divine Chimaera. Providence sponsored his deeds, and even the king of Lycia was forced to believe in his divine descent. But Glaucus knows how fitfully the gods favor men: Bellerophon became hateful to all the gods and wandered alone, "avoiding the track of human beings"; and two of his children fared worse: Ares killed Isandrus, and Artemis in anger slew Laodomeia. And yet all their fates were supernatural; Glaucus' ancestors were not ordinary mortals. Thus Glaucus himself, looking back on his past, partly proves that men are like leaves, and partly tries, as he bolsters himself, to astonish Diomedes.[38] If he cannot claim that he is a god, at least he has divine

31. *Iliad* 6. 119–129; *Odyssey* 6. 149–153.
32. Cf. *Iliad* 9. 134 with 276; 21. 150; consider *Odyssey* 7. 208–212.
33. But cf. Basset, *CP* xviii, pp. 178–179.
34. Cf. *Iliad* 5. 128–132, 827–828.
35. *Iliad* 6. 146.
36. Cf. 21. 462–466, where Apollo speaks.
37. *Iliad* 6. 152–211.
38. Cf. Aeneias' speech to Achilles, *Iliad* 20. 200–241, where he recites his lineage; note the frequency of *anthrôpoi* and of superlatives (204, 217, 220, 233); the gods are absent (144–152).

ancestors. And Diomedes, who before had such contempt for the genealogies of Pandarus and Aeneias,[39] now finds an excuse to break off the combat. As his grandfather Oeneus entertained and exchanged gifts with Bellerophon, so he and Glaucus should exchange their armor and proclaim themselves "ancestral friends."

Axylus, a friend to strangers, dies; Glaucus and Diomedes, whose grandfathers were friends, agree to separate. Axylus had no divine protection, while Glaucus had its shadow, a divine lineage. In his lineage are the gods, whose presence then can save Glaucus (or Diomedes) even now. By calling up his past – made glorious by heaven – Glaucus reminds Diomedes that the gods control, morally and physically, the actions of men. He holds up, as a desperate shield, the flimsiest providence; but Diomedes, no more anxious than himself to fight, jumps at his offer. Their ancestral friendship replaces the gods, who are, more remotely, their ancestors.[40]

When Hector has returned to Troy and bid his mother pray to Athena, he curses Paris: if the earth swallowed up Paris and he saw him descending to Hades, Hector would forget his sorrow.[41] Hector's wish before, though just as vehement, that he be without offspring and die unmarried,[42] Paris' cowardice had warranted; but now, whether he shirks or not, Hector longs for his death. Zeus Olympius raised Paris as a bane to the Trojans, for Zeus Olympius is gone.[43]

Everyone feels the absence of the gods. When Helen had heaped scorn on Paris' strength, he falsely attributed his defeat to Athena: "Now Menelaus has won a victory with the help of Athena, but I another time shall be victorious over him; for there are also gods on our side."[44] Another time he will be victor, whenever the gods so wish it. Although he then was wrong about Menelaus, he was right about himself – Aphrodite did save him – so it seemed reasonable to suppose that some god had protected Menelaus. His mistake was justifiable. But now not even he thinks the gods make for victories: *nikê d'epameibetai andras.*[45] Victory alternates between men: who knows why? No longer Aphrodite but Fortune is his goddess: Athena has just refused the Trojans' prayer.[46]

Helen feels despair more deeply than Paris. Priam had kindly received her on the ramparts of Troy; and she, provoked by his kindness, had burst out

39. *Iliad* 5. 244–256.
40. Cf. *Iliad* 6. 229 with 230, 235.
41. *Iliad* 6. 280–285.
42. *Ibid.* 3. 40, cf. 56–57.
43. *Ibid.* 6. 282–283.
44. *Ibid.* 3. 439–440; cf. 4. 7–12.
45. *Ibid.* 6. 339.
46. *Ibid.* 6. 311–312.

with: "Would that death had been pleasant to me when I followed your son to Troy."[47] But now, though Hector has not even spoken to her, her sense of guilt is even greater: on the very day she was born, not on the day she committed her crime, she wishes to have died; but, she adds, the gods decreed otherwise.[48]

Hector leaves Helen and Paris, and meets his wife Andromache with his son Scamandrius. They form a beautiful but gloomy scene. Despair finally overtakes Hector; he predicts the fall of Troy: "Well I know this in my mind and my spirit, that there will be a day when sacred Ilium will perish, both Priam and his people."[49] What Agamemnon had foretold, when Pandarus wounded Nienelaus, Hector has come to believe, and in the very same words prophesies: but Agamemon saw Zeus, shaking his dark aegis, as the cause of Troy's capture.[50] Hector sees nothing. The future is black: the gods have deserted.[51]

The absence of the gods has made the sixth book the darkest in the *Iliad,* and we can now better understand how the gods interfere in the heroic world. In the *Iliad* providence makes a difference; it is despotic and can either enhance or nullify a hero's virtue; but in the *Odyssey* it is kind and just (except for Poseidon, a benign ogre), and it never interferes with merit but only assists it; none of the gods favors the suitors. War and peace differ most in this. In peace failure is man's own responsibility,[52] for the gods have less at stake and exert little influence. In war the heroes become puppets of the gods, and submit to a fate beyond their control: necessity sets the course and is the prevailing wind. And yet men still remain responsible: this is the theme of the *Iliad* and the tragedy of Achilles.

47. *Ibid.* 3. 173–174; cf. 24. 763–764.
48. *Ibid.* 6. 345–349; cf. 3. 180 with 6. 344.
49. *Ibid.* 6. 447–449.
50. *Ibid.* 4. 163–168; cf. 127–129.
51. Note the frequency of *daimonie: ibid.* 6. 326, 407, 486, 521, cf. 318; 7. 75.
52. *Odyssey* 1. 32–34.

Chapter II
The Plot of the Iliad

Hector and Paris re-enter the battle in the seventh book, appearing like a fair breeze that a god sends to tired rowers and after some success on their part, Athena and Apollo agree to stop the war for a day, and let Hector challenge an Achaean to a duel.[1] Helenus, a prophet, intuits the plan of the gods, who do not openly show themselves but assume the shape of vultures, and remain, as in the sixth book, invisible to men.[2] Hector is pleased with his brother's proposal, and offers to fight anyone whom the Achaeans might choose as their champion; he also promises, if he should kill his opponent, to give back the corpse for burial, so that a mound may be built near the Hellespont, "and someone of later times, sailing by in a large ship over the wine-faced sea, may say: That is the tomb of a man who died long ago, whom excellent though he was, glorious Hector killed': so someone will say, and my fame shall never die."[3]

Hector wants immortal fame. Though he believes that Troy will be taken, he wants a monument to be left behind for himself.[4] It shall perish, he shall live on. The gloom of the sixth book, brought on by the gods' absence, is dispelled in the seventh by the light of a future glory. Hector finds his way out of a godless present in his fame to come. Fame is despair's remedy. If the gods are gone, if they no longer care, then men must take care of themselves; they must adopt a surrogate for them, and Hector suggests what the Achaeans reluctantly accept, immortal fame. Instead of being dependent on the gods, they will become dependent on other men *(anthrôpoi).* They will snatch from the very uncertainty of war a permanent gain. No matter who will be victorious, and regardless of the justice of their cause, both sides can win glory. They can share in the success of their enemy, and even find a certain satisfaction in being killed.

The difference between the combat of Menelaus and Paris, that took place a few hours before, and the present contest of Ajax and Hector, indicates the

1. *Iliad* 7. 1–42.
2. *Ibid.* 7. 43–61.
3. *Ibid.* 7. 87–91.
4. Cf. *Iliad* 6. 444–449.

great change in the character of the war. Menelaus fought with Paris to settle the war, Ajax and Hector fight in a trial of prowess. They fought to decide the fate of Helen – who would be her husband? – Ajax and Hector fight without any regard for Helen, but only to determine who is the better warrior. They exchange threats and boasts; Menelaus and Paris fought in silence. They were in deadly earnest, while Hector and Ajax can break off their combat and give each other gifts in parting. Menelaus had wished to accept Hector's challenge, but Agamemnon (with all the other kings) restrained him,[5] for though he was the right opponent against Paris, he would have now lost his life to no purpose. He is no longer the champion of his own cause. Had Menelaus killed Paris, he would have recovered Helen; if Hector now wins, the Achaeans would recover Ajax' corpse, which would serve, once it was buried, as a memorial to both Ajax and Hector. Fame and renown would seem to be as precious to Hector as Helen is to Menelaus, and his new ambition so much inflames him that he can refer quite brazenly to the Trojans' perfidy.[6] Whatever oaths they may have broken, whatever injustice they may have done, has no relevance now. As long as Helen was at the center of the dispute, the Trojans were in the wrong; but now that she is discarded, and becomes merely a theme for heroic exploits, right and wrong no longer apply. *"Publica virtutis per mala facta via est"* ("The public way of justice is through crimes").

As the cause of the war has changed, so also have the central characters. Helen unleashed a war over which she loses control. The war, having worked loose from its origins, now feeds itself: the desire for Helen generated the desire for fame, but the offspring no longer acknowledges the parent. There can now be no other end to the war than the destruction of Troy. The restitution of Helen will no longer suffice. Diomedes speaks for all the Achaeans when, in answer to the Trojans' proposal (of returning all the stolen goods except Helen), he says: "Now let no one accept either the goods of Alexander or Helen herself; for even a fool would know that the ends of destruction have already been fixed for the Trojans."[7] Not even if the Trojans give back Helen would the Achaeans stop fighting. The war has passed out of her hands and become common property. No longer is the war petty. It has transcended the bounds of its original inspiration and assumed the magnificence of heroic ambition. Paris and Menelaus now have minor roles, Helen is scarcely mentioned.[8] She was a necessary irritant that has become superfluous, and Helen herself knows this. "Upon myself and on Paris," she tells Hector, "Zeus has placed an evil fate, so that we might be the theme of song among men

5.   *Iliad* 7. 104–107.
6.   *Ibid.* 7. 69–72, cf. 351–353.
7.   *Ibid.* 7. 400–402.
8.   Cf. *Iliad* 11. 122–142.

(anthrôpoi) who shall be."[9] Not herself but her fame justifies the war: in the perspective of later generations can be found her own *raison d'etre*. What gives purpose to the quarrel is not a present victory but a future fame. In the third book Helen was weaving into a cloak many contests of the Achaeans and Trojans, "who for her sake suffered at the hands of Ares."[10] As the war had been staged for her benefit, she had gone up on the walls to watch her two husbands, Menelaus and Paris, fight for her; but now an impersonal fame has overshadowed any personal pleasure, although she may still find some comfort in a future glory. Her pleasure has become more remote and less immediate: nothing that can be woven into cloth or that can be seen. She is the plaything of the future (of her own renown) and no longer manages her own destiny.[11] She is caught up in a larger issue and concedes her own insignificance. And Menelaus, like Helen, realizes the change which Hector proposes, for he berates the Achaeans and calls them "spiritless and fameless in vain,"[12] since they are not eager to accept Hector's challenge; for unless they are animated by fame his challenge is meaningless. They must disregard Menelaus and look to themselves. Their own aggrandizements, not Menelaus' vengeance, must become their aim. As their ambition, in becoming more selfish, becomes more grand, so their prowess, in advocating immortal fame as its end, can at last justify itself.

Socrates once derived the word *hêrôs* ("hero") from *erôs* ("love")[13] and though it is a jest, it is metaphorically true. The heroes, or their ancestors, are the offspring of gods who fell in love with mortals; and they retain in themselves a divine longing, which is not just confined to physical desire, though that is its origin,[14] but which prompts them to a transcendent hope, that turns their only weakness into their best resource. If they are fated to die, if they are barred from becoming immortal in deed, their death can ensure them a fictional immortality. Were a goddess to fall in love with them again, they could only continue an heroic line; but were they to turn aside from a hopeless quest, and rely on themselves, they would be assured of a deathlessness unaffected by the gods *(oiothen oios,* "all alone').[15] War absorbs into itself the desire they have for self-perpetuation (after Helen left Sparta, she became barren);[16] for it unites their virtue with their ambition, so that, in displaying the one, they satisfy the other. And if we are not repelled by allegory, no better image for

9. *Iliad* 6. 357–358.
10. *Ibid.* 3. 125–128.
11. Cf. *Iliad* 6. 323–324.
12. *Iliad* 7. 100.
13. Plato *Cratylus* 398c 7–d5.
14. Cf. Plato *Symposium* 206cl–209e4.
15. *Iliad* 7. 39, 226; cf. 6. 1; 11. 401.
16. *Odyssey* 4. 12–14.

the *Iliad* could be found than the fable told by Demodocus, about the adultery of Aphrodite and Ares and its detection by Hephaestus. Here is all the horror and glory of war in secret agreement with the desires and delights of love, which the threads of art, more subtle than a spider's web, bind together and reveal.

Homer has carefully prepared the shift from Helen to fame as the cause of the war, a shift that the magical disappearance of Paris first indicates. When victory is almost within Menelaus' grasp, as he drags Paris toward the Achaeans, Aphrodite breaks the strap by which Menelaus held him, and "snatching Paris away, she hid him in a great mist, and set him in the sweet-smelling bridal chamber."[17] Paris is as effectively dead as if he had been killed. Overcome by desire for Helen, he is indifferent to fame: if Athena gives victory now to Menelaus, the Trojans' gods at another time will aid him.[18] He becomes isolated from the war, which now begins again without him. Although his original injustice began the war, it continues by the injustice of Pandarus, which serves as the transition between the recovery of Helen and the desire for fame. Not Paris but Pandarus wounds Menelaus. Paris disappears, and the responsibility for the war spreads among the Trojans, while among the Achaeans Menelaus remains the central figure, about whom they still rally. But he too disappears in the seventh book, when Agamemnon persuades him not to accept Hector's challenge.[19] To transform pettiness into grandeur, a private quarrel into a public war, may require injustice; but once the transformation is completed, once both sides accept the new conditions, the demands of justice no longer apply.

> Were it not glory that we more affected
> Than the performance of our heaving spleens,
> I would not wish a drop of Trojan blood
> Spent more in her defense. But, worthy Hector,
> She is a theme of honor and renown;
> A spur to valiant and magnanimous deeds,
> Whose present courage may beat down our foes,
> And fame in time to come canonize us.[20]

The change that takes place among the heroes finds its echo among the gods. Aphrodite saved Paris, but Diomedes in the fifth book wounds her, and she never reappears among men. Even as Paris, a man wholly dominated by desire, disappears, so Aphrodite, the divine principle, as it were, which gives

17. *Iliad* 3. 369–382.
18. *Ibid.* 3. 439–440.
19. *Ibid.* 3. 126–128. 7. 104–107.
20. Shakespeare *Troilus and Cressida* 2. 2. 195–202.

him most support, retires, and leaves the war to Ares and Apollo, Athena and Hera.[21]

After the contest of Ajax and Hector, Nestor proposes that a trench be dug and a wall built as a protection for their ships and themselves.[22] The kings agree, and while they are laboring at the wall, the gods, seated by Zeus, admire their work, and Poseidon speaks among them: "Zeus father, what mortal on the boundless earth shall still disclose his plans to the immortals? Do you not see how the Achaeans have built a wall for their ships and run a trench about it, but they have not offered famous hecatombs to the gods? Its fame will go as far as the dawn scatters light, and they will forget the wall that I and Phoebus Apollo built for the hero Laomedon."[23] Poseidon fears that the fame of the Achaeans' wall will outstrip the fame of his own wall. He interprets the wall as an insult to the gods. Fame is not a concern of the gods: they can neither hinder nor advance it. Not even the destruction of the wall, which Homer describes,[24] prevents us from hearing of it. As long as the war concerns the quarrel which Hera and Athena had with Paris,[25] the gods are the ultimate authority; but as soon as the war turns away from Paris and embodies the desire for fame, the gods seem unnecessary. Just as Hector attempted to break loose from them, in challenging an Achaean to a duel, so Nestor takes up his suggestion and proposes the building of tomb, trench, and wall. Hector was unsuccessful, for he does not kill Ajax. Nestor succeeds for a time, but even his attempt is thwarted by the gods. The wall would make the Achaean camp as permanent as Troy: should they win or lose, it would remain as a record of their siege. Nestor improved on Hector, for victory was the price of his fame, while Nestor relies on a collective effort that disregards prowess as well as success. The wall is the most glorious attempt to break out of the gods' influence, and it fails. But Zeus helps them along in their belief, for he forbids in the eighth book any intervention by the gods in the war.[26] In the fourth book Hera was given *carte blanche* to do what she wanted, but now that her personal revenge has been transcended, Zeus no longer will brook any interference.

The desire for fame enhances everything. The shield of Nestor, "whose fame reaches heaven," and the "curiously-wrought breastplate of Diomedes, which Hephaestus had fashioned" become the objects of Hector's ambition.[27] These unknown arms become desirable in the light of fame. Everything is

---

21. Cf. *Iliad* 5. 330–333, 348–351, 427–430.
22. *Iliad* 7. 337–343; at 342 the vulgate *hippon* would be merely a mistake arising from *laon;* cf. 18. 153, where cod. A has *laoi* superscriptum.
23. *Ibid.* 7. 446–453.
24. *Ibid.* 12. 10–33.
25. *Ibid.* 4. 31–33; 24. 27–30.
26. *Ibid.* 8. 7–22.
27. *Ibid.* 8. 191–197.

worth acquiring if fame is the goal. Teucer is encouraged and urged on by the offer of a tripod or two horses or a woman, if Troy is captured.[28] Teucer, who plays no role in the fifth book and is mentioned once in the sixth, becomes in the middle books an important figure. And in the same way, Glaucus and Sarpedon, Idomeneus and Meriones, become more important. Everyone joins in the desire for fame.

Once the transition has been completed to the second cause of the war, Homer begins to lay the foundations for the third cause. It is now in the eighth book that Zeus outlines the death of Patroclus and the return of Achilles.[29] Even as the disappearance of Paris announced the shift to the second cause, so Zeus' prophecy indicates the final cause. Thus three causes underlie the *Iliad:* Helen first, fame second, and Patroclus third. From personal revenge to impersonal ambition and back again to revenge is the *Iliad's* plot. The love for Helen turns into the love for fame, which in turn becomes Achilles' love for Patroclus. From *erôs* to *kleous erôs* ("love of fame") to *erôs* is the cycle of the *Iliad:* but how Achilles' eros unites the other two will be our final problem.

---

28. *Ibid.* 8. 287–291, cf. 285 with 9. 133.
29. *Ibid.* 8. 473–477.

Chapter III
The Embassy

Agamemnon calls an assembly of all the Achaeans, where he proposes in earnest what he had once used as a test of their resolution; and yet now they hear silently the same speech which before had upset them and induced them to return home.[1] Their roles are reversed; Agamemnon wishes as much to flee as the Achaeans had wished before, and they now seem as determined to stay as Agamemnon had been intent on capturing Troy. Agamemnon, however, has changed his speech in two respects; he no longer addresses the Achaeans as a whole (though they all are present) but only their leaders, and he omits to say how shameful their flight would appear to future generations.[2] What now keeps the Achaeans seated, though they are troubled in their hearts,[3] is the desire for immortal fame. The plague and the withdrawal of Achilles had so broken their spirit that not even the prospect of disgrace had then dissuaded them; but now, even though Agamemnon fails to mention it (for fame no longer attracts him), they are inclined to stay. As long as Agamemnon wished to capture Troy, the ignominy of his return was paramount; but his despair now makes him ignore what has inflamed everyone else. Even as Menelaus had been replaced by Ajax, so Agamemnon, once his brother's suit lost its importance, had to yield his own preeminence. He knows that the Achaeans will not obey him, that the darkness of the night as well as their new ambition will check them. He hands over to the Achaean kings the business of the war. He is as ready now to humble himself before Achilles, as prompt on the morrow to be wounded and remain out of action for the rest of the *Iliad*.[4] Thus Diomedes can openly assert Agamemnon's weakness,[5] for Agamemnon has already abandoned his pretensions to power, now certain that no one will question his authority. Were Helen their object, his force must equal his rank, so that the Achaeans may be obliged to avenge an abstract wrong that does not affect them; but if their appetites are engaged, if immortal fame is now their object, so that defeat would seem a personal disgrace, Agamemnon can afford

1. *Iliad* 9. 18–25 = 2. 111–118; 9. 26–29; cf. 2. 139–141.
2. *Ibid.* 9. 17; 2. 110, 119–138.
3. *Ibid.* 9. 4–8.
4. Cf. *Iliad* 11. 276–279.
5. *Iliad* 9. 37–39; cf. Part I, Chap. IV above.

to forego an absolute sway and be content with the titular superiority. Diomedes can bid him depart as brusquely as he himself once ordered Achilles to return home, and be as confident as Agamemnon once was that the others will stay behind.[6] Even without Agamemnon the Achaeans cohere and stick together: he has become superfluous. But fame is so much more an inducement than justice, that Diomedes goes even farther than Agamemnon ever did: the others can also depart, he and Sthenelus will win alone. Thus he usurps the power of Agamemnon and replaces Achilles as the emblem of virtue.

Nestor, in partly approving of Diomedes' rebuke of Agamemnon, assigns to him the leadership of the war (of the young), while he reserves for Agamemnon his authority in the council (among the kings).[7] He distinguishes between the sceptre and the fist of Agamemnon, and thus prepares the way for his reconciliation with Achilles. But although he is willing to grant Agamemnon's weakness before the whole assembly, he does not wish to propose before them the embassy to Achilles; for if they remain ignorant, they can always count on Achilles' future support, but if they know (as Achilles hopes),[8] its success would compromise Agamemnon, and its failure would deprive them of hope. Were Achilles to re-enter the war, Agamemnon would be forced, in admitting his error, to surrender his sceptre, whereas Diomedes can excel Agamemnon by night (the Doloneia) without being his rival by day: he is wounded soon after him in Book Eleven; but should Achilles refuse to return, the Achaeans, in losing their mainstay, would also lose heart. Nestor knows that Diomedes' nocturnal prowess will not seriously affect Agamemnon's authority; but he fears that an Achilles, able to support his ambition by day-time deeds, would disturb again the hierarchy of command. Achilles must be coaxed by something other than the return of Briseis, something that no longer will allow him to threaten Agamemnon, nor show up his own pride as petulance. And that bait is immortal fame.

Nothing more clearly reflects the changed purpose of the war than the embassy to Achilles. It offers the Achaeans their best chance to reconcile Achilles with Agamemnon. If Hector had not made his challenge, the embassy would have been impossible. Only on this new basis can the Achaeans hope to persuade Achilles to forget his wrath, and be aroused by a new ambition that affords greater scope to his fury. If Helen has disappeared as the cause of the war, Briseis should also lose her importance. If the stake is now immortal fame, and the conflict is indifferent to Menelaus' just complaint, then Achilles' quarrel with Agamemnon, who as unjustly provoked him as Paris did Menelaus, should be resolved in favor of this larger issue. An indivisible

6.   *Ibid.* 9. 40–46; 1. 173–175.
7.   *Ibid.* 9. 53–75.
8.   *Ibid.* 9. 369–372.

trophy, immortal fame, will replace the division of spoils. What would always lead to disputes, the petty arithmetic of how much each man is worth, will vanish before a more generous calculation, whose scales are no longer in the hands of Agamemnon but of all mankind. The exact weighing of virtue in the coinage of booty becomes contemptible, and what is beyond measure, immortal fame, is now set up as its standard. Achilles is to be lured by honor: he can forgive Agamemnon because Agamemnon can never again dishonor him. Merit would be the only guide to reward, and, in spite of Agamemnon's jealousy, Achilles would receive his due. Let Agamemnon deprive him of all material gain: it can only please for a lifetime, and Achilles in the future will so much the more be recompensed. Achilles' fame lies beyond the touch of envy: if he can now show himself magnanimous, the authority of Agamemnon will yield before his own power. Agamemnon must rely on gifts and bolster his rank by the arbitrary display of his will, but Achilles can trust in the present to his might and to his deeds in the future. The quibbles on their relative positions among the Achaeans will not arise in the face of Achilles' future superiority. Agamemnon can irritate Achilles, but Achilles' revenge is assured. As long as Achilles looks to Agamemnon for satisfaction, no number of gifts can disguise Agamemnon's false position, nor persuade Achilles to relinquish his claim to Agamemnon's sceptre; but if he can only look beyond this temporary injustice, his ascendancy to come his own virtue guarantees. Agamemnon's sway extends no further than the narrow circle of the Achaean camp, and his every act of aggrandizement is bought at the price of a future ignominy; while every accommodation by Achilles to his mean tyranny will only increase his reputation and add lustre to his name. Achilles' dangerous ambition, to rule over all the Achaeans, can be diverted into a safer and more glorious end. To render him harmless as well as more worthy of himself prompts the Achaeans to send the embassy: that Achilles cannot bring himself to accept their offer, and that he cherishes more deeply his present humiliation than a lasting fame, all this makes the beginning of his tragedy.

The embassy prayed to Poseidon that they might easily convince the great heart of Aeacides *(megalas phrenas Aiakidao)* "whom they found pleasing his heart *(phrena terpomenon)* with the clear-toned lyre – beautiful it was and intricately wrought, and it had a silver bridge – he chose it from the spoils after he had sacked the city of Eetion, and with it he was pleasing his spirit *(thymon eteroen)* and was singing the famous deeds of men" *(klea andrôn).*[9] Achilles as Aeacides, as the grandson of Aeacus, sings the deeds of famous heroes. In taking up the lyre he puts on his ancestral self: as he finds his pleasure in the past, he becomes part of the past and loses his present identity. Excluded from action, he sings of the actions of others; he consoles his inactivity by rejoicing in others' prowess; and wrapped up in their past, he lives

9.   *Ibid.* 9. 184–189.

more by his own past than by himself. Achilles remained by the ships, and though "he never visited the ennobling assembly *(agoran kydianeiran),* nor ever went to war, yet he was destroying his spirit, and kept on longing for the battle-cry and war."[10] His self-imposed idleness still chafes him. His absence from the war has not diminished his desire. Even the assembly seems a place to win glory: *kydianeira* ("bringing glory") is used elsewhere only of battle, but Achilles, now that he is cut off from all action, sees even in speaking a certain prestige. As he cannot share in present deeds nor in present counsel, he cannot hope for a future fame. He is isolated from the present and the future, and so only the past exists as something which cannot be taken from him. He sacked the city of Eetion – no one can deny it – but the witness to his virtue is this lyre, which testifies as well to his failure; for it gave him an instrument more suited to a blind Demodocus than to an Achilles. He celebrates the deeds of others, but others should celebrate his own. The lyre cannot satisfy him, for he is now forced to please himself instead of having others please him. His pleasure is in another's fame and not in his own. *Klea andrôn* ("the famous [deeds] of men") stand one remove from *erga andrôn* ("the deeds of men"); they are the reflection of virtue, not virtue itself; and Achilles, in singing of another Achilles, becomes the shadow of what he was. In becoming a minstrel, he has become unwillingly an *anthrôpos;* in withdrawing from the war, he deserts his own character. If martial excellence is denied Achilles, he no longer is Achilles, no longer what he thinks and we think he is. His name depends on his deeds, and he cannot abandon all deeds without forfeiting himself. In becoming passive, he loses that which distinguished him: "idleness is the corruption of noble souls."[11] But it was the very source of his actions, his *megalopsychia* ("greatness of soul"), which had made him withdraw and betray his former self. And the tragedy of Achilles lies here: what made Achilles destroyed Achilles. As soon as he reflects, he is lost, and he is bound to reflect, to pick up this lyre, once he stops fighting. If he ever doubts the worth of what he has been trained to do, he will destroy himself. Any check to his outer action will turn all that force upon himself. His sword needs an object, and if it is wanting, it will be himself. When the embassy arrives, he is ripe for persuasion.

When Odysseus has enumerated the gifts Achilles will receive, if he puts off his rage, he tells Achilles that "even if Atreides is hateful to your heart – he and his gifts – take pity at least on all the other forlorn Achaeans, who will honor you like a god: surely you might have great honor among them, for now you might slay Hector, who in his murderous lust would come quite near you, since he says no Danaan, whom the ships brought hither, is his equal."[12]

10. *Ibid.* 1. 490–492; cf. 9. 440–443.
11. BT Scholiast 1. 490; cf. *Iliad* 18. 104–110.
12. *Ibid.* 9. 300–306.

Odysseus is quite willing for Achilles to reject Agamemnon's gifts, but he tries to irritate Achilles by repeating the boast of Hector, even though Hector did not mention him but Diomedes.[13] Achilles is right to reject Agamemnon's gifts, for though the gifts acknowledge Agamemnon's need of Achilles, they do not admit Achilles' superiority. Not only do they gloss over his challenge to Agamemnon's rank, but they aim to restore Agamemnon's predominance. Agamemnon has put a price on Achilles' worth; he has calculated his equivalence in terms of so many horses and so much gold, and were Achilles to accept them, he would be accepting Agamemnon's estimation of himself. If he is reducible to a cipher, he must submit to Agamemnon's domination. He would not acquire a greater rank, were he to allow "more" to mean "better"; for then he would acknowledge Agamemnon's right to settle his worth: but he had withdrawn his support originally because Agamemnon had presumed to decide what he could and could not have. To accept the gifts is to accept Agamemnon's authority; and what is more, to receive seven Lesbian women, whom he himself had captured,[14] would humiliate himself. In giving them to Agamemnon, Achilles was the arbiter of Agamemnon's worth; in giving them back, Agamemnon would usurp his own position. Were then Achilles to acknowledge Agamemnon's equation, and confound numerical superiority with natural greatness,[15] his whole attack on Agamemnon's position would fail.

Even as the catalogue of ships was intended to confound number with strength, and thus whole peoples are mentioned who never reappear in battle (for example, the Rhodians and Arcadians), so now Agamemnon's generosity gives a limit to Achilles' excellence, and half his promises can never be put to the test. Achilles will not live to enjoy the spoils of Troy, nor will he be able to claim Agamemnon's daughter, nor the seven cities below Pylos. Not even if his daughter rivaled Aphrodite in beauty and Athena in skill, would Achilles marry her.[16] He could not. Only if he returns now to his father's home, could he hope to marry; only his withdrawal now would assure him the wealth Agamemnon so vainly promises; only in Phthia would he live with the ease he cannot have in the future if he stays.

Agamemnon wished to reestablish his position prior to Achilles' withdrawal, to forget his injustice so that Achilles might forget his weakness, and to reduce Achilles' attack on his authority to a mere outburst of temper. But once the gap between them has been opened, no appeal that seeks only to restore Achilles' former status can bridge it. Once Achilles has seen how valuable he is, he will never be content with less than complete domination. If

13. *Ibid.* 8. 532–538.
14. *Ibid.* 9. 128–130.
15. Cf. *Iliad* 2. 123–133.
16. *Iliad* 9. 388–391.

Achilles had not retired from the war, he would have never known if he was as great as he assumed, nor would the Trojans have ventured to fight in the plain, nor would the Achaeans have built their wall. His wrath freed the war from a static siege, where the worth of each hero could never be tested, and turned it into a precise measure of excellence. Achilles' absence from the field lets Diomedes and Ajax, Hector and Sarpedon come forward, and make the frame, as it were, within which we must see Achilles, when he at last reappears. The random sorties, that had made up so large a part of the war[17] have now given way to a full-scale war, a war for immortal fame. It is this new kind of engagement Achilles is asked, but cannot bring himself, to join; nor is he asked so much for the sake of Agamemnon (or Menelaus or Helen) but because of Hector, who can now become the measure of Achilles' prowess, which no longer has to be weighed by the amount of booty he receives. Achilles, however, refuses to consider the war as changed, but prefers to gloat over Hector's success rather than accept it as a challenge.[18] He takes for granted what is by no means so certain, that he is better than Hector.[19] He does not see the war as anything other than what it was. He is indifferent to immortal fame.

Achilles had already protested against the war in the first book, saying that he had not come to fight because of the Trojans, who had neither driven off his horses nor plundered his land, but to obtain redress for Agamemnon and Menelaus.[20] Achilles had been fighting in an alien war, a war he had joined more out of lack of any other attraction than out of a deep-seated feeling to see justice done. He was willing to stay, if his prerogatives were respected, and if nothing occurred that more affected him. But Agamemnon, in taking away Briseis, had not only dishonored Achilles, but also had made Briseis herself more desirable than she was. She may not be worth fighting over,[21] yet she is the equal of Helen, who could not be dearer to Menelaus than Briseis to Achilles.[22] If the Achaeans fight for Helen, he asks the embassy, why should not he fight for Briseis? If Agamemnon leads so great an expedition to recover so small a prize, why should not he desert a war that can bring him no satisfaction and has already brought him disgrace? As long as Achilles hammers away at the pettiness of the war, he is perfectly justified; and yet he fails to see the change he himself brought about. Achilles is careless of immortal fame. Although he mentions it as a choice his mother gave him, it does not move him; although his return means the loss of his fame, he still considers it

17. Thucydides i. 11.
18. *Iliad* 9. 348–355.
19. Cf. *Iliad* 7. 113–114; 20. 434–437.
20. *Iliad* 1. 152–160.
21. *Ibid.* 1. 298–299.
22. *Ibid.* 9. 337–343.

a possibility.[23] His fame and his return are balanced for him, as if they were equal alternatives; and they *are* nicely poised if one has the chance, like Achilles, to reflect upon them. He had not at first thought there was an alternative. He had resigned himself to a short life,[24] but his enforced idleness made him reflect. To choose immortal fame demands a certain blindness to the pleasures of life, of which Achilles, in his very minstrelsy, has become aware. Life seems more worthwhile than a bloodless renown.[25]

Achilles, in having no care for the Achaeans, loses all care for his fame. Their destruction and his ignominy seem minor losses. He cannot pity them unless his "name" has greater weight than himself. Achilles believes in the absoluteness of his virtue: it does not need to be put into action, nor does the opinion of others measure it. He wishes to enjoy his virtue alone,[26] without performance and without regard for others. He does not need to use his virtue in order to prove himself virtuous. What Shakespeare's Odysseus tells him, he does not believe,[27]

> That no man is the lord of any thing,
> Though in and of him there be much consisting,
> Till he communicate his parts to others;
> Nor doth he of himself know them for aught,
> Till he behold them formed in the applause
> Where they're extended; who, like an arch, reverberates
> The voice again; or, like a gate of steel
> Fronting the sun, receives and renders back
> His figure and his heat.

Achilles finds his applause not in earth but in heaven, where Zeus honors him. When Phoenix warns him that it would be baser *(kakion)* to defend burning ships than to receive Agamemnon's presents now,[28] he replies, "I think that I am honored by the will of Zeus" *(phroneô de tetimêsthai Dios aisê).*[29] He can disregard the honor he would have from the Achaeans, because he has a greater honor from Zeus. Achilles sets Zeus higher than immortal fame. What the Achaeans and Trojans have tried to escape from, the arbitrary decrees of the gods, Achilles trusts completely. He does not find them arbitrary, for they are mere extensions of himself: they are his surrogates. In neglecting human affairs, in thinking he can decide when to interfere and when not, Achilles is

23. *Ibid.* 9. 410–416.
24. *Ibid.* 1. 352.
25. Cf. *Odyssey* 11. 489–493.
26. *Iliad* 11. 762–763.
27. *Troilus and Cressida* 3. 3. 115–123.
28. *Iliad* 9. 601–605, Cf. 249–250.
29. *Ibid.* 9. 608.

elevated to a god. He despises the promises of Odysseus, that the Achaeans will honor him like a god, for he believes that Zeus (his Zeus) has bridged that "likeness," and transformed it into a complete identity. Achilles is a god. He wears the ring of Gyges. He does not heed the advice of his mortal father,[30] nor of those who are dearest to him: Phoenix, Odysseus, and Ajax.[31] He has cut all his ties with mortality but one. Patroclus is the flaw in his presumed perfection, and is the silent witness to his own doom. The true subject of the embassy is not Agamemnon and his gifts, nor even immortal fame, but Patroclus.

Achilles is given the cruelest choice: immortal fame, but without the enjoyment of a living renown, or a present luxury and ease, but without fame. Hector could challenge Ajax because he knew he would not die.[32] Immortal fame was something in the future and not what would at once ensure his death. Euchenor knew he would perish if he went to Troy, but he knew as well he would die of a cruel disease if he stayed at home.[33] He chose the more glorious end, and shunned not a peaceful old age but a painful death. And Adrastus did not believe his father, who prophesied his death at Troy.[34] Achilles is quite different from Adrastus, Hector, or Euchenor. Unlike Adrastus he believes his mother, unlike Hector his prowess will certainly end in death, and unlike Euchenor he could enjoy his kingdom. If Achilles were not Achilles, the choice would never arise, for his wrath lies outside the will of Zeus, and it was the pause in the fighting which his wrath afforded that made the decision acute; but insofar as Achilles is Achilles (that is, virtuous) there can only be one answer, to elect immortal fame. And yet Achilles decides too late, when, no longer willingly, he reenters the war. He is forced by necessity, as he himself admits,[35] and that necessity is Patroclus' death. Achilles decides not by himself but by another. Patroclus makes his decision for him. He wanted to be absolute, but he discovers that it entails the death of his companion. In trying to escape all dependence on other men, he sends to his death Patroclus. When he at last returns to the war, he no longer fights for immortal fame, though he may deceive himself into so believing,[36] but to avenge Patroclus, and that vengeance is what Phoenix had called baser and less honorable than acceptance of Agamemnon's gifts.[37] But before we look at this final stage, we must

30. *Ibid.* 9. 252–259, 438–443.
31. Cf. *Iliad* 9. 197–198.
32. *Iliad* 7. 52–53; cf. 20. 337–349.
33. *Ibid.* 13. 666–670.
34. *Ibid.* 2. 830–834.
35. *Ibid.* 18. 113; 19. 66.
36. *Ibid.* 18. 121.
37. *Ibid.* 9. 601–605.

first look at an absolute Achilles, an Achilles most clearly revealed in the speech of Phoenix.[38]

After Phoenix has pledged his loyalty to Achilles, he inserts the story of his life most casually. "I would not wish to be left apart from you," he tells Achilles, "not even if a god himself would promise to scrape off my old age and make me a blooming youth again, such as I was when I first left Hellas, with its beautiful women;" after which he tells how his mother begged him to sleep with his father's concubine, and when his father learned of it, how he cursed him and called upon the Furies to make his son childless, which, Phoenix adds, "the gods, Zeus of the dead and Persephone, fulfilled."[39] Phoenix recites this as if the mere remembrance of his youth sufficed to recall his entire past, and yet it retells, though ambiguously, Achilles' own action, and weighs the right and wrong of his wrath. Achilles bitterly allows Agamemnon, in spite of his promised oath, to sleep hereafter with Briseis,[40] and, with that assumed, Phoenix can draw the parallel between his own story and Achilles'. Phoenix, insofar as he slept with his father's concubine and was cursed by Amyntor, and insofar as the curse was fulfilled by Zeus, is like Agamemnon, who will soon sleep with Briseis, was cursed by Achilles, the curse to be fulfilled by Zeus. If the conflict between Agamemnon and Achilles is seen as similar to that between a father and his son, where, strangely enough, Achilles assumes Amyntor's and Agamemnon assumes Phoenix' role, we cannot tell who was right and who wrong; but Phoenix goes on to say, in lines that Plutarch alone has preserved,[41] that he considered killing his father, was restrained by one of the gods, and finally left home and came to Phthia.[42] And likewise, Agamemnon dishonored Achilles (by taking away Briseis), even as Amyntor dishonored his wife and son (by having a concubine); and Achilles would have killed Agamemnon, just as Phoenix would have killed his father, had not Athena restrained him; and again, having withdrawn from the war, he intended to return home. Phoenix then is also like Achilles. His dishonor, his wrath, his murderous intent and its check, his escape from home,

38. I do not enter into the "discrepancies" in Phoenix' speech: they are less important, even if they do exist, than its purpose.
39. *Iliad* 9. 444–457.
40. *Ibid.* 9. 336–337.
41. *Ibid.* 9. 458–461 are found in his *de aud. poet.* 8 (459–460, also in *Coriolanus* xxxii, and 461 in *de adul. et amic.* 72b), where he says Aristarchus excised them out of fear: scholars are divided as to whether they are genuine or not; cf. G.M. Bolling, *The External Evidence for Interpolation in Homer*, pp. 121–122 (with bibliography); G. Pasquali, *Storia della Tradizione*, pp. 231–232; Bolling in *The Athetized Lines of the Iliad*, pp. 26–27, tried to refute Pasquali (unsuccessfully, I believe).
42. *Iliad* 9. 462–480.

all correspond to something in Achilles' own past. Phoenix has presented a complex story, so that Achilles may have the best of both roles. As an outraged father or a dishonored son, as Amyntor or Phoenix, Achilles is justified; but Phoenix, by telling it in such an offhand way, wishes to warn Achilles that his grievance is now past history, that already he has obtained as much vengeance as could be wished, and that, if he persists, he will destroy himself. The loyalty of Phoenix to Achilles should serve as a model for Achilles, of what he owes to Patroclus: for the gods protected Phoenix in his youth, but he would not now accept their aid even if they promised to make him young; just so Achilles, who has been favored by Athena and Zeus, should not now look to them for assistance. Meleager's story, then, is the condemnation, as Phoenix' own was the justification, of Achilles. It is introduced expressly as a warning to Achilles, and as Phoenix had summarized the books before the embassy in his own life, so now he foretells the subsequent events of the *Iliad* in the story of Meleager.[43]

The high-spirited Aetolians were defending the city of Calydon against the Couretes, and as long as Meleager fought, things went badly for them; but when he became angry at his mother and stayed at home, the attackers began to succeed, and the elders of the Aetolians, promising a great gift, beseeched Meleager to return; his father, mother, and sisters urged him, but only when his wife Cleopatra recounted how many sorrows befall a captured city, did he pity the Aetolians and re-enter the war.[44] It is not difficult to see how this corresponds to the plot of the *Iliad*, but the most important point, I think, has not been noticed: the situation is completely reversed. Meleager is not one of the Couretes but one of the Aetolians: he is not attacking but defending Calydon; and not his friend but his wife persuades him to forget his wrath. Meleager is Achilles, the high-spirited Aetolians are the high-spirited Trojans, and Cleopatra is Patroclus.[45] Achilles then is a Trojan, and even as Patroclus' name is reversed in Cleopatra,[46] so the whole story presents a mirror-image of the events at Troy. Achilles has become, in his wrath, an exile; he has turned into an enemy, not just an observer, of the Achaeans; he has changed his allegiance and become enrolled as a Trojan ally. He is a Trojan outside the walls, a Hector enraged. The Trojans could have appealed to Hector, as the Aetolians did to Meleager, by recounting the human sorrows that would attend a captured Troy;[47] but the Achaeans could not move Achilles except by pointing to a silent Patroclus. If Hector had withdrawn from the war, and had Priam, Casandra, Hecuba, and Andromache beseeched him to return, Phoenix' story

43. Cf. BT Scholiast 9. 527; W. Schadewaldt, *op. cit.,* pp. 139–143.
44. *Iliad* 9. 528–600.
45. Cf. *Iliad* 9. 351–355, 551–552.
46. E. Howald, cited by Schadewaldt, *op. cit.*, p. 140.
47. Cf. *Iliad* 6. 407–439.

would exactly correspond; but their very absence in Achilles' case lays stress on his isolation, and shows how close he has come to an inhuman self-suffi-ciency. Hector could be as much Meleager as Achilles is; but he is a civil Achilles, an Achilles who has not lost *aidôs* ("shame"); and yet in all else he resembles him, so that this first meeting between them, as it were, in the realm of an old fable, marks the first stage in their ultimate identity.

Agamemnon had ended his speech of reconciliation thus: "Let Achilles submit – Hades is implacable and unconquerable, and therefore he is the most hateful of all the gods to mortals;"[48] and though Odysseus quite reasonably omits it when he addresses Achilles, yet he replaces it by promising him that he will be honored like a god.[49] He somehow suspects Achilles' divine preten-sions, and Phoenix more openly, when he urges Achilles to relent because the gods themselves are not inexorable, "whose virtue, honor and power are greater, numbers Achilles among the gods.[50] Agamemnon and Phoenix try to persuade Achilles by example, and as their choice of Hades and the gods depends on what they think would seem convincing to Achilles, we can read-ily measure his ambition by his refusal. Achilles wants to be absolute; he almost succeeds. He has forced himself into a posture that can admit (and ask) no quarter. He thinks himself alone, splendidly alone, and though Patroclus proves him wrong, his conviction lasts long enough to seal his doom. As long as he believes in his own uniqueness he is as monstrous as the Cyclops. What is metaphorically true in the *Iliad* becomes a fabulous reality in the *Odyssey*.[51] Both live alone: Polyphemus actually, Achilles by belief. Both cultivate and consult only their *thymos*.[52] Both are huge *(pelôrios)*: Polyphemus is so huge that the stone which blocks his cave not even two and twenty wagons could move; Achilles is so huge that three Achaeans had to bolt and unbolt the door to his tent.[53] If Polyphemus were killed, Odysseus would never be able to leave the cave; if Achilles were killed, the Achaeans would never take Troy.[54] War is like the cave of the pastoral Cyclops, from which none escape but by the un-willing help of its denizen. Polyphemus must be blinded so that Odysseus may escape, Achilles must lose Patroclus so that Hector may be killed. Polyphemus devours the companions of Odysseus, Achilles wishes his angry strength would allow him to devour Hector.[55] Thus Polyphemus is one extreme of Achilles' character, as his immortal horses are the other: one the embodiment

48. *Iliad* 9. 158–159; cf. 1. 177 = 5. 891; consider 9. 312–313.
49. *Ibid.* 9. 302–303.
50. *Ibid.* 9. 497–501.
51. Cf. Part I, Chap. IX above.
52. *Iliad* 9. 255, 496, 629, 675; *Odyssey* 9. 278; cf. Eustathius on *Odyssey* 1. 69; 9. 183; 16. 31.
53. *Iliad* 24. 453–456; *Odyssey* 9. 240–243.
54. *Odyssey* 9. 302–305; cf. *Iliad* 9. 458–459.
55. *Iliad* 22. 346–347; cf. 24. 409; *Odyssey* 9. 291.

of the animal, the other of the thing. Achilles is called merciless, and he has a merciless heart *(nêlêes êtor),* and only Polyphemus is also said to be so *(nêlees thymos)*[56] Polyphemus is wild and untamed *(agrios)*; so is Achilles.[57] The Cyclopes are lawless *(athemistoi),* not because they do not lay down laws each to his own family, but because they do not have regard for one another, that is, they lack civil shame.[58] Achilles likewise gives commands among his followers but has no regard for Agamemnon's decrees.[59] Polyphemus boasts that he does not pay attention to Zeus; Phoenix warns Achilles that he does not regard the Litai.[60] Polyphemus then is the brute perfection of Achilles, Achilles without weakness, without Patroclus. He is what Achilles wants to but luckily cannot be. He shows what a monstrosity is bred out of disobedience to order, no matter how arbitrary that order may seem. He is almost Homer's final verdict on Achilles, whose disrespect for Agamemnon, though a trifle, unleashed a fury that sweeps Achilles on to his own death.

> Then everything includes itself in power,
> Power into will, will into appetite;
> And appetite, an universal wolf
> So doubly seconded with will and power,
> Must make perforce an universal prey,
> And last eat up himself.

56. *Iliad* 9. 497, 632; 16. 33, 204; *Odyssey* 9. 272, 287, 368; cf. Part I, Chap. VIII above.
57. *Iliad* 9. 629; 21. 314; 22.313; *Odyssey* 2. 19; 9. 215, 494; cf. *Odyssey* 9. 118–119; *Iliad* 6. 97–101; 24. 41; *agrios* is also used of battle, fire, and Athena's wrath (*Iliad* 17. 398, 737; 4. 23).
58. *Odyssey* 9. 106, 112–115, 215, 269, 274–278.
59. *Iliad* 9. 97–99.
60. *Iliad* 9. 510; *Odyssey* 9. 275.

Chapter IV
The Deception of Zeus

Achilles acts like a god, but Patroclus makes him forfeit that likeness. Though he suppresses nature, it finally betrays him in the shape of his friend: *naturam expelles furca, tamen usque recurret* ("You may expel nature with a pitchfork, yet it will always return"). His imitation of immortality cannot last: Patroclus stops it. But the gods whom Achilles imitates, do they too have their Patroclus? Are they too subject to a power beyond their art? Homer gives us his answer in the so-called "deception of Zeus."

When Hera sees Poseidon in disguise urging the Achaeans to battle, she thinks of a plan to end the war quickly: to put on a disguise that will deceive Zeus. She enters her chambers, made by her son Hephaestus, the lock on whose doors no other god but herself could open, and adorns herself as artfully as possible.[1] Then, taking aside a guileless Aphrodite, Hera begs of her: "Give to me love and desire, by which you overpower all immortals and mortal men."[2] Her excuse is that she wishes to reconcile Oceanus, the "genesis of the gods," and Tethys, who have been at strife with one another, and for a long time have not slept together, ever since "wrath fell upon them."[3] Aphrodite grants her request and gives her a magical girdle, "wherein there was love and desire and persuasive speech, that is wont to steal away even the mind of the prudent."[4] Having put on this girdle, Hera goes to the brother of Death, Hypnos, the "king of all gods and all men."[5] If he will lull to sleep Zeus, she promises, he will receive a golden throne and a footstool, made by her son Hephaestus.[6] Hypnos at first refuses, protesting that he would even put to sleep Oceanus – *hos per genesis pantossi tetuktai* ("he who is the genesis for all") – but not Zeus, unless he himself so wished it; and reminding Hera how he had deceived Zeus once before, when Heracles sailed home from Troy, and had not Night saved him – "queen of gods and of men" – Zeus would have cast him into the sea.[7] Hera deprecates his fear: Zeus does not care as much

1.   *Iliad* 14. 153–186.
2.   *Ibid.* 14. 198-199.
3.   *Ibid.* 14. 200–210.
4.   *Ibid.* 14. 216–217.
5.   *Ibid.* 14. 233.
6.   *Ibid.* 14. 238–241.

for the Trojans as he had for Heracles; and she changes her reward: anyone of the Graces shall be his bride.[8] Hypnos then agrees, if Hera will be willing to swear an oath,[9] and once she is sworn, he accompanies her to Olympus where Zeus surveys the Thasians and Mysians.[10] Coming into the presence of Zeus, while Hypnos assumes the shape of a bird, Hera's beauty dazzles Zeus, and he wishes to sleep with her at once.[11] Hera, however, "thinking guile," says it would be shameless to sleep out in the open, where anyone might see them: would it not be better to retire to her own chamber, which her dear son Hephaestus had made?[12] At last Hera's plan is discovered: she wished to lure Zeus into her chamber, whose lock no one but herself could open; and once locked in, Zeus would have to submit to her terms, and the Trojan war would come to an end. And yet she cannot persuade Zeus (in spite of her girdle), for his desire admits of no delay. They sleep together, and "under them the divine earth sprouted fresh grass, the dew-drenched lotus, the crocus, and the delicate hyacinth."[13] Thus Hera is foiled by nature. Even as Hypnos would not accept her proposal, as long as she offered him the throne of Hepaestus, so Zeus' passion outstrips her guile. She had hoped to enlist natural powers, sleep and desire, into the services of art: to entice Zeus by the charms of Aphrodite and hold him by the craft of Hephaestus. She believed that nature would submit to art, but she ought to have known, when Hypnos rejected the throne made by Hephaestus, that art must submit to the passions, that the superiority of art is ephemeral, and that nature will always triumph. Thus the deception of Zeus is a failure.[14]

If then Hera fails to deceive Zeus, it is not surprising (as some have thought it is) that Poseidon does not help the Achaeans more than before; for Hypnos, who is as guileless as Aphrodite, did not know what Hera had intended, and, thinking her plan a success, goes of his own accord to tell Poseidon.[15] The Achaeans are entitled to no more than a short respite. Their

---

7.   *Ibid.* 14. 242–262.
8.   *Ibid.* 14. 264–268; cf. BT Scholiast 270.
9.   *Ibid.* 14. 271–276; cf. 15. 36–38; Aristotle *Met.* 983b 30–33.
10. *Iliad* 13. 1–6.
11. *Ibid.* 14. 280–328; cf. 3.442–446.
12. *Ibid.* 14. 329–340; cf. BT Scholiast 338.
13. *Iliad* 14. 347–348.
14. Some may object to my applying the terms "nature" and "art" to Homer, as if he thought so abstractly; but if it be kept in mind that I understand by nature that which always acts in the same way and is indifferent to us, even though the gods may try to coerce it, the distinction is clear: the heroes appeal to the latter but not to the former, who are gods that cannot be apostrophized (thus the winds do not hear Achilles, *Iliad* 23. 194–195); and from the gods' point of view, Sleep and Night are at the service of all, since by themselves, having no human offspring, they do not take sides.
15. *Iliad* 14. 354–360.

leaders succeed in routing the Trojans, until Zeus awakens and forces Poseidon to retire from the war.[16]

Sleep, Desire, and Night have equal powers over gods and men, and only Death, the brother of Sleep, is man's peculiar fate. Mortality distinguishes men from the immortal gods. It makes the gods, who are free from death, the masters of men. Although they are subject like men to sleep, desire, and night, yet their immortality grants them one advantage: they are not forced to be moral. The gods have the ring of Gyges, which allows them to do whatever they wish without regard for the consequences. If they sometimes feel responsible for their charges, they help them; but if they ignore the heroes, they never pay for their neglect. If they choose to be as arbitrary as Achilles, they will never feel as guilty as he, after he has sent Patroclus to his death. Ares is easily soothed by Athena when he hears of his son Ascalaphus' death:[17] the revengeful grief of Achilles cannot be solaced. Mortality puts a limit to Achilles' irresponsibility, not only by checking his aggrandizement but also by forcing him to admit that he can lose something more precious than his own life. His virtue cannot stand alone; for even when he thinks he is self-sufficient, he relies on the gods; and this reliance becomes so great that in the end he can do nothing unless they assist him. Achilles thought he was closer to Zeus than to Agamemnon, but when Zeus denied his prayer that Patroclus return alive, he discovered his ties with *anthrôpoi* were stronger than his claim to immortality. When Sarpedon rushed against Patroclus, and Zeus pitied them both, undecided whether he should save Sarpedon or not, Hera dissuaded him, and Zeus quite readily resigned himself to the loss of his son;[18] while Achilles, who imitated his indifference (as he relied on his protection) could not bring himself to accept the death of Patroclus. He feels compassion more strongly than a god ever can. His natural affections outstrip his self-taught principles. His indifference crumbles. He comes to see himself as more the son of Peleus than the son of Thetis, more human than divine. Cyclopean Achilles, an automaton of enormity, puts not only himself but all heroes on trial. His experiment in immortality is disastrous, for it depends on a providential world, a world that the gods must always take care of. Achilles sums up heroic virtue, and shows that its price is eternal providence. *Pantes de theôn chateus' hêrôs.*

16. Cf. *Iliad* 14. 14–15 with 15. 7–8.
17. *Iliad* 15. 113–142.
18. *Ibid.* 16. 431–461.

Chapter V
Patroclus

Patroclus was much affected by Nestor's appeal, and, as soon as he returned to Achilles, forgetting to report what he was charged to find out,[1] begged Achilles to reenter the war:[2]

> *ainaretê, ti seo allos onêsetai opsigonos per, ai ke mê Argeioisin aeikea loimou amerêis?* (accursed [or dreadful] in your virtue, how will another even yet to be born have profit from you, if you do not ward off shameful ruin for the Argives?)

Achilles' virtue is accursed and dreadful, for no one in the future (let alone now) will take pleasure in or derive benefit from it, unless he prevents an unseemly disaster. Patroclus warns Achilles, as Phoenix had warned him before, that he is gambling away his fame as he holds stubbornly to his virtue. What Nestor had said, that Achilles would enjoy his virtue alone – *oios tês aretês aponêsetai*[3] – Patroclus takes to mean the loss of immortal fame. Agamemnon had pleaded with Achilles (through Odysseus) to help Agamemnon; Odysseus on his own account had pleaded with him to help the Achaeans; Phoenix had pleaded for him to help himself; and Patroclus to help posterity. He can be as isolated in the present as he wants, if he will display toward the future a ghostly beneficence; but were he to abstain from all action, his untested virtue would deny him all fame. Achilles insists so much on immediate honor, to compensate for his early death, that he ignores the danger of a lasting infamy. He wishes to enjoy now, in fact, what posterity can only grant him in fancy, to gather into the present moment all of the future. He cannot balance, against his conscious perfection, a promised glory. Although he has threatened to leave, he must stay, so that the defeat of the Achaeans may sustain his intense awareness of his own virtue. Indeed he would even wish for the death of all Achaeans and Trojans, were he and Patroclus to escape (being neither Achaean nor Trojan), "in order that we might alone destroy the sacred heights of Troy."[4] He does not think on the barrenness but merely on the self-

1. *Iliad* 11. 611–615.
2. *Ibid.* 16. 31–32.
3. *Ibid.* 11. 763.
4. *Ibid.* 16. 100; but cf. 17. 404–407; 20. 26–27.

sufficiency of such a triumph, which would make him at last the absolute master of his own honor.

When Odysseus reported Achilles' refusal to Agamemnon, he only mentioned Achilles' threat to depart at dawn, and not his milder answer to Ajax, that he would not consider "bloody war" before Hector would come to the ships and tents of the Myrmidons.[5] The parable of Meleager had made Achilles slightly modify his threat; but the change is useless. Were Hector to succeed in breaking through the wall, Achilles' belated action might save himself, but it would not help the Achaeans, whom Hector would attack, not on Achilles' flank, but on Ajax'. Achilles had speciously moderated his stubbornness, so that he might flatter himself by his own good nature, and yet remain as adamant as before. As the Achaeans are given impossible conditions to fulfill, should they wish to appease Achilles, Achilles can persevere in his own conceit and at the same time pretend his willingness to relent. He can compromise without compromising himself. He can regret his obduracy but keep his wrath.[6] He can send out Patroclus, in all righteousness, without his yielding at all, and can thus ensure his return, which the Trojans might otherwise hinder, if they set fire to his ships.[7] He will obtain honor from all the Achaeans, as well as Briseis and glorious gifts, even though he will not have submitted to Agamemnon.

Achilles carefully avoids any mention of the embassy, as he now understands what Phoenix had meant, when he warned him that to accept Agamemnon's gifts, if the ships are already burning, would not only be baser but entail less honor.[8] He now admits what he could not foresee, that "it is impossible to cherish anger continuously."[9] But having admitted that, he cannot bring himself to confess his error. He must re-enter the war, and yet he must maintain the absoluteness of his own virtue, but not compromise his chance of returning home. And Patroclus' request, that he be allowed to put on Achilles' armor, gives him the almost-perfect solution. He will not go himself but will send a surrogate, who is the mere extension of himself. Patroclus will be mistaken for him, and thus he can rout the Trojans without ever leaving his tent. But one thing upsets him: suppose Patroclus, this inanimate toy, suddenly is fired by his own ambitions? Suppose his success will be too brilliant and involve Achilles in a greater dishonor?[10] Were Patroclus to do more than assure the return of Briseis, and either kill Hector or capture Troy, Achilles

5. *Ibid.* 9. 650–655, 682–683.
6. *Ibid.* 16. 61–63; cf. P. von der Muehl, *Kritisches Hypomnema zur Ilias,* pp. 241–242.
7. *Iliad* 16. 80–82.
8. *Ibid.* 9. 600–605.
9. *Ibid.* 16. 60–61; cf. 4. 31–33.
10. *Ibid.* 16. 87–90; cf. 22. 205–207.

would be eclipsed by the very instrument of his design. Patroclus might become independent of Achilles; he might be able to achieve what none of the other Achaeans had been able to do, freedom from Achilles' tyranny. Achilles might find that his armor was superior to himself, that the weapon and not its owner guaranteed success, and that his own renown could accomplish more than his own prowess. His fears are unfounded: Patroclus does not excel him: but he also fails to return. And his failure to return, the one flaw in Achilles' scheme, sets the stage for Achilles' own tragedy.

Patroclus puts on Achilles' armor, but leaves behind Achilles' spear, which no one could wield except Achilles.[11] Automedon yokes Xanthus and Balius to the chariot, and puts between the traces the blameless Pedasus, a horse Achilles had taken when he sacked the city of Eetion, "who even though mortal followed immortal horses."[12] A three-horse chariot is elsewhere unknown to Homer. Why then should Patroclus add a mortal horse, that at best would be superfluous and at worse a hindrance, to the two immortal horses of Achilles? "Homer wishes to show us," the BT Scholiast remarks, "the nature of the hero, that it is composed of the mortal and immortal." Quite true; but why should Homer wish to insist on such a point now? His meaning goes deeper. Even as Patroclus is Achilles' one tie to humanity, and with his death dies Achilles' pity,[13] so Pedasus is Patroclus, whose death reveals how impossible it is to yoke together, as Achilles had wished, the rights of divinity with the duties of men. Pedasus is a mere appendage to these immortal horses, Patroclus is nothing but the trace-horse of Achilles; but the wounded Pedasus can more easily be disentangled from his reins than the dead Patroclus discarded by Achilles. Patroclus was to be only an extension of Achilles, while his death, though it cuts him off completely, binds him more closely to Achilles than he ever was bound in life. Pedasus was a blameless horse, not only because his excellence ranked him with Xanthus and Balius but also because he was not responsible for his death; and Patroclus likewise is blameless,[14] his virtue being almost the equal of Achilles' and his death Achilles' fault. Achilles' share of mortality dies with Patroclus and Pedasus, and all that remains of him is the immortality of his horses.

Homer speaks to Patroclus throughout his *aristeia,* as if he somehow felt responsible for him and wished to console him for the harshness of his fate. Not his prowess nor his victories but his ineluctable death enlists Homer's sympathy: "Whom first, whom last did you kill, Patroclus, when the gods called you to death?"[15] Homer had spoken to Menelaus when his life was in

11. *Ibid.* 16. 130–144.
12. *Ibid.* 16. 145–154.
13. Cf. *Iliad* 21. 100–105.
14. *Iliad* 17. 10, 379; 23. 137.
15. *Ibid.* 16. 692–693 (cf. 5. 703–704; 11. 299–300), cf. 16. 20, 584, 744, 754, 787, 812, 843.

danger, or when he thought his petty triumphs should be celebrated;[16] and it is not accidental that he, who shares so little in heroic ambition, and Patroclus, who is so little responsible for his fate, should be the two persons whom Homer most often addresses. The plot involves them, one at the beginning, the other at the end: but the plot is not their own doing. Patroclus' death follows so quickly on the heels of his success, that no one, except Achilles, moves so much under the spell of doom. And yet the doom of Achilles is part of his destiny (it is almost self-made); Patroclus' death is alien to Patroclus and belongs more to Zeus and Achilles than to himself; so Homer, in calling to him, seems to stand beside him and to be in at the kill, lest Patroclus, without the gods and without Achilles, feel himself completely abandoned.

Zeus was undecided whether he should save Sarpedon or not, and later he could not decide whether Hector should die;[17] but he had no doubts about Patroclus. The death of Sarpedon was arbitrary; he could have survived Patroclus. The death of Hector was in itself unnecessary; it could have been otherwise. Both are heroes without a fixed destiny; not everything they do leads to one end; they can repeat themselves. But Patroclus could not be reprieved: not because his death arose from an inner necessity (and in this he resembles Sarpedon and Hector), but because his death was the trigger to Achilles' death. It foreshadowed another's death, a death that could not be avoided. It set off another's tragedy. That no god protests the fate of Patroclus indicates that none will protest Achilles'.

---

16. *Ibid.* 4. 127, 146; 7. 104; 13. 603; 17. 679, 702; 23. 600.
17. *Ibid.* 16. 433–438; 22. 168–176; cf. 20. 277–299.

Chapter VI
Achilles and Patroclus

If Menelaus had always seemed to cut a poor figure, whether he worsted Paris or volunteered to fight Hector, he more than makes up for it after the death of Patroclus. His efforts are sustained and his exploits prodigious. He shows as much concern for Patroclus' corpse, says Homer, as a mother would feel for her first-born calf.[1] But what is he to Patroclus, or Patroclus to him, that he should be spurred on to such virtue? He does not act so much out of some regard for Patroclus, as because he feels his own interests are at stake. He sees that the war has re-adopted its original character. As he had gone to war to avenge the rape of Helen, so Achilles will re-enter the war to avenge Patroclus' death. A private quarrel will become once again the main theme of the *Iliad*. Achilles will fight for Helen.[2] When Menelaus' love for Helen had been transmuted into the desire for glory, he had lost his importance, handing over to others the conduct of the war;[3] but as soon as Achilles' love for Patroclus will shape the rest of the *Iliad*, Menelaus reassumes, as a sign of Achilles' return, his abandoned role. Almost spent is the ambition with which Hector had inspired the heroes, while the desire for vengeance, which had initiated the war, returns once again as its cause. The combat of Achilles against Hector and that of Menelaus against Paris have more in common with each other than with the contest between Ajax and Hector. They are in earnest, while Hector and Ajax competed for glory. They are provoked by hatred, while Hector could exchange gifts with Ajax. They are the rightful champions of their own cause, while Ajax was picked by lot and Hector could have been Aeneias. And yet the central part of the *Iliad,* which dealt with the love of fame, does affect the struggle between Achilles and Hector. Achilles is not merely Menelaus nor is Hector merely Paris, but Achilles unites Menelaus with Ajax (the personal vengeance of one with the impersonal ambition of the other), while Hector retains the role he played against Ajax, even though he takes on some features of Paris. Ajax and Menelaus join in protecting the corpse of Patroclus, and thus indicate how the first two parts of the *Iliad* come together in the end. We must now see how Achilles puts off his wrath and re-enters the war.

1.   *Iliad* 17. 4–6; cf. BT Scholiast 16. 7–11; 17. 133–137.
2.   *Iliad* 19. 324–325; cf. 9. 337–339.
3.   Cf. Part II, Chap. II above.

When Achilles had prayed to Zeus, that Patroclus push back the Trojans to the city as well as that he return safely to the ships, Zeus granted the first request and denied the second;[4] and this new plan of Zeus', which Thetis failed to report,[5] marks the first rupture between Achilles and Zeus. As long as Thetis had told him what Zeus intended, Achilles could not fail to believe in his own power; nor, as long as the Trojans continued to triumph, could he doubt the infallible result of his prayers. He is indeed pious Achilles. Never had he made a move without the assistance of a god, whether Athena had checked his impulse to kill Agamemnon, or Thetis had answered his appeal for revenge; so he persuaded himself that they would never desert him, and he could afford to dispense with his mother's intervention. He treated the gods as if they were under his thumb and were as obedient to his whims as he had hoped Agamemnon would be. Achilles, who thought himself the master, becomes the slave of the gods. He cannot live without them. He must live miraculously.

Patroclus is absent longer than Achilles expected, and he begins to recall what Thetis had once told him, that the best of the Myrmidons would die, while he was still living.[6] Although he had known about this prophecy, he had forgotten it in his haste to obtain satisfaction, and free himself honorably from his own intransigence; and since his convenience advised him to ignore it, he so much the more easily could plead his forgetfulness. And yet Achilles' memory is a strange mixture: he could keep fresh the injury dealt him by Agamemnon, but he could not remember the fate of Patroclus. Even he is uneasy, uncertain if he dispatched Patroclus in good faith; for in repeating now his admonition to Patroclus, he proves his innocence by slightly changing his warning: "I charged him to return to the ships," Achilles says to himself, "when once he had averted the baneful fire, (and I charged him as well) not to fight against Hector."[7] But he had not told Patroclus to avoid Hector. He did forbid him to attack Troy, lest Apollo might rout him, but he now omits the baser motive which had dictated his concern – his fear that Patroclus might achieve more glory and honor than himself[8] – and substitutes for that the pretense that he had warned him about Hector. Indeed, in his prayer to Zeus, he actually referred to Hector as Patroclus' opponent: "In order that even Hector

4. *Iliad* 16. 241–252.
5. *Ibid.* 17. 404–411. The iterative *apangelleske* (409) determines the sense of *dê tote ge* (410), which bears its normal meaning: a return to the immediate present after a stated time in the past (Ameis-Hentze); and it does not mean, as it is usually taken, that Thetis never told him, which contradicts 18. 9–11; in *Odyssey* 22. 185–186 *phoreeske* serves the same purpose (cf. *Iliad* 20. 408–411). Cf. how the iteratives in *Iliad* 1. 490–492 explain *ek toio* in 493.
6. *Iliad* 18. 9–11.
7. *Ibid.* 18. 13–14.
8. *Ibid.* 16. 87–94.

will see if our comrade knows how to battle alone."[9] These are not the words of someone who can truthfully say he warned Patroclus; but they are the words of an Achilles who deliberately forgot the doom of Patroclus, so that his own pride could be appeased. Perhaps "deliberately" is not too strong an indictment, but his guilt is there. He is not innocent of Patroclus' death, nor is he in turn completely responsible. He stands, like all tragic heroes, an ambiguous trial tortured by the doubt of his innocence, as he protests the consciousness of his guilt. He shares his guilt with Hector, who is, as it were, his agent; but he also shares Hector's innocence, who merely carried out the will of Zeus. His fury against Hector far exceeds the fury of an innocent man. He exacts from Hector the penalty he feels that he himself should pay. He attempts to drown in the slaughter of Trojans the growing sense of his own guilt. He expresses both his innocence and his guilt, his grief at the loss of a friend and his pain at being his murderer, when he tells his mother, *ton apôle-sa*,[10] which can mean "I lost him," as Achilles now intends, or, what he finally comes to believe it means, "I killed him." The murder of Patroclus was not Achilles' aim, but the casual consequence of his wrath. He had delegated his shadow of himself, dressed in his own armor, to vindicate his honor. He had not so much been desirous for Patroclus' death as he had been anxious for himself. He was careless of Patroclus because he was certain of his success; but his certainty was more a necessary hope to further himself than a proved conviction that it would not harm Patroclus.

As soon as Achilles learns of Patroclus' death, "a black cloud of grief engulfed him," and he throws himself upon the ground, *megas megalôsti tanystheis keito* ("mightily in his might, he lay stretched out"), as if he were dead. His captured slaves surround him and utter cries of lament, and Antilochus fears he will commit suicide, "severing his throat with iron."[11] Achilles' muttered wailings are heard by his mother who, when all her sisters are gathered round her, laments the imminent death of her son,[12]

> *ô moi egô deilê, ô moi dysaristotokeia*
> ("Ah me, wretched that I am; ah me, unhappy bearer of the best
> of men.")

Accompanied by the tearful Nereids, she leaves his father's cave, and standing near Achilles takes his head in her hands. It has often been noticed that all of this scene resembles a funeral, and that it signifies the death of Achilles.[13] The phrase *keito megas megalôsti* ("he lay mightily in his might")

9.   *Ibid.* 16. 242–244.
10. *Ibid.* 18. 82.
11. *Ibid.* 18. 22–34.
12. *Ibid.* 18. 54.
13. Cf. J. Kakridis, *Homeric Researches,* pp. 65–75.

was used of Cebriones' death,[14] and far from being a blemish was purposely planted there to explain its occurrence here. Achilles is dead. *Keiso megas megalôsti* ("You lay mightily in your might"), Agamemnon tells him in Hades, "and your mother came out of the sea, whom the immortal Nereids followed."[15] Thetis holds Achilles' head just as he will hold the head of the dead Patroclus, and Andromache, Hecuba and Priam that of Hector.[16] With the death of Patroclus, Achilles himself dies. "I honored him above my companions," he tells Thetis, "equal to my own head."[17] Patroclus is Achilles' head, and his death has cost Achilles his own.[18] He is now no more than a corpse. He stays alive by the nectar and ambrosia Athena gives him: the very medicine Thetis gives the dead Patroclus and Aphrodite the dead Hector, so that their bodies might not decay.[19] Achilles' and Hector's ambition, to be immortal and ageless, is finally granted them; they obtain the elixir of immortality,[20] one when he is dead, the other when he wishes that he were. Achilles belongs to the world of the dead, and his every action will seem as mechanical as a somnambulist's, and as ineffectual as a dream.

Achilles is a work of art. He has more affinities with the golden hounds of Hephaestus than with the natural elements in his own lineage. His denial of nature is his constant attempt to break out of mortality. Hence it is only fitting that the eighteenth book should open with a catalogue of the Nereids and end with the making of his shield.[21] The Nereids represent all that he refuses to acknowledge, the superiority of nature over art; and the shield proclaims all that he wants to be his, an ordered and fabricated world. The shield is surrounded by Oceanus,[22] placed at the limits of man's nature, and beyond which it is impossible to go. Ocean is the only one of the gods that does not obey Zeus' summons, when he calls all of them to assemble.[23] He is the only one beyond Zeus' power. Hera had pretended she could reconcile Ocean with Tethys, but she never does; Hypnos had pretended he could lull him to sleep, but he never does; and Achilles pretends that Zeus is stronger than the Achelous, but he only briefly succeeds.[24] Hephaestus conquers the Xanthus,

---

14. *Iliad* 16. 776.
15. *Odyssey* 24. 39–48.
16. *Iliad* 23. 136–137; 24. 712, 724.
17. *Ibid.* 18. 81–82, cf. 114; 23. 94.
18. *Kephalê* ("head") sometimes means *psychê* ("soul," "life"), and I suspect it means so here (*Iliad* 4. 162; 17. 242; cf. *Odyssey* 2. 237 with 3. 74). cf. *Odyssey* 2. 237 with 3. 74.
19. *Iliad* 19. 38–39, 352–354; 23. 185–187.
20. *Odyssey* 5. 196–199.
21. *Iliad* 18. 39–49.
22. *Ibid.* 18. 607–608.
23. *Ibid.* 20. 4–9.
24. *Ibid.* 21. 194; cf. Part I, Chap. IX, X; Part II, Ch. IV above.

so that the Olympian gods, who make the heroic world providential, may dominate the *Iliad*. The gods appear on the shield in the city of war, but they are absent in the city of peace:[25] so it is not by chance that the gods are less active in the *Odyssey,* nor that Odysseus travels to the end of Ocean, where Hades is, the absolute end of man.[26] Heroes live in a poetic world, a world where accident has almost vanished, and everything takes place according to fate. Providence is chance unblinded. The gods are *technai* ("arts"), who correct the faults of nature: but they are a small part of the whole. They beautify the whole, and as war is uglier than peace, they play a greater role in the *Iliad* than in the Odyssey. Achilles needs them; without them he is a Cyclops; with them he just manages to be noble. Achilles dies in Book Eighteen. He dies when the providential world on which he depended breaks down; but he is resurrected by art and goaded on by the gods for the rest of the *Iliad*. He cannot help the Achaeans until he is rearmed: the despoiling of Patroclus has stripped himself. He is refitted by Hephaestus, so that he may take his revenge; but it is merely a concession of the gods, merely a fiction of Homer's, merely a sop to Achilles. He becomes a puppet, who performs his ghostly motions by a kind of inertia. The display of his virtue comes too late: he cannot redeem, no matter how great his slaughter, the virtue he lost in sending Patroclus to his death. Achilles is Achilles because he is a warrior, but before he was willing, and now he is compelled. He has lost his will. "Truly it is not base," Thetis tells him, "to ward off destruction from your wearied companions";[27] but it is not noble either. Achilles becomes a contrivance, a thing, a work of art. He has lost that greatness of soul which, ironically, he more displayed in his anger against Agamemnon than now in his revenge on Hector. He becomes more hateful to himself than Hades ever was.[28] He becomes his worst enemy.

Before Achilles arms himself for battle, he is reconciled with Agamemnon; but one must not take Agamemnon's self-humiliation as the vindication of Achilles. Agamemnon can afford to be abject because Achilles cannot now dispute his authority: he is too busy defending himself from his own guilt to make any demands on another. Achilles had compared himself to Heracles, "whom fate and the cruel anger of Hera conquered, and so even I, if there is made a like fate for me, shall die."[29] Achilles begins here his self-deception. He must omit in his own case the anger of Hera that was partly the cause of Heracles' death; for it was not the wrath of a god but his own wrath that sealed his fate. He tries to return to where he was before his wrath, when he was *ôkymorôtatos allôn* ("doomed to an early death beyond all others"),[30]

25. *Iliad* 18. 516–519, 535–540.
26. *Odyssey* 10. 508–515; 11. 12–22.
27. *Iliad* 18. 128–129; cf. 9. 601–602.
28. *Ibid.* 9. 312–314.
29. *Ibid.* 18. 119–120.

and he had had no doubt that he would die at Troy. His wrath then became his fate, taking over his external destiny and making it his own. He brought himself to do through his own action what fate had planned in advance. He becomes free of fate only to become enslaved to his own character. Vainly he tries to restore a fateful world, where he would no longer be responsible. What Agamemnon does so brazenly in the defense of himself (excusing his own folly on the grounds of Zeus'),[31] Achilles also does; but he is more subtle than Agamemnon as his sense of guilt is much stronger. He wishes that Briseis had perished when he sacked Lyrnessus,[32] as if Briseis were to blame and not himself, or as if he could not have found another pretext for his wrath. He wishes that strife and anger had perished among gods and men,[33] so that he would not have been able to err. He shows himself indifferent to the gifts of Agamemnon,[34] as if he had never cared for honor and was always careless of rewards. He longs to go to war without eating, as if he had never feasted when the Achaeans were dying.[35] "The Achaeans cannot mourn a corpse with their bellies," Odysseus tells Achilles, "for too many die day after day, one after the other: when could one cease from toilsome fasting? But we must bury him who dies and weep for a day, having a pitiless heart."[36] Achilles must have a pitiless heart *(nêlea thymon)*, and Achilles once did have a pitiless heart: when he had neither fought nor wept for the dead.[37] His pitiless heart had kept him from the war, and his softened heart has made him return. When he should have showed his mildness, he preferred to be hard; when he should now show his hardness, he must be mild. His responsibility to Patroclus is too oppressively his own burden for Patroclus to be numbered among the other dead. Achilles tries to redeem his innocence by fasting, as if physical privation would show his inner loss, but by fasting he only stands condemned.

30. *Ibid.* 1. 505, cf. 417–418.
31. *Ibid.* 19. 86–136.
32. *Ibid.* 19. 59–62.
33. *Ibid.* 18. 107–108.
34. *Ibid.* 19. 147–148.
35. *Ibid.* 9. 225–230.
36. *Ibid.* 19. 225–229.
37. Cf. Part I, Chap. VIII above.

Chapter VII
The Exploits of Achilles

Achilles begins his exploits in the twentieth book, and Homer addresses him by his father's name, "son of Peleus," for with his return to the war he becomes like his father. He takes over again the office which Agamemnon had filled in his absence: the Achaeans now arm around him as they once were ordered to arm by Agamemnon.[1] Achilles now enters the war with eagerness: *akorêtos,* "insatiate," Homer calls him. The Trojans take fright as soon as they see him, "swift-footed Peleion ablaze in his armor, equal to mortal-destroying Ares."[2] His virtue, his patronymic and appearance are enough to warrant a simile, that also the presence of the gods justifies.[3] He is known to the Trojans as the son of Peleus (by his father's name) and as swift-footed (by his special virtue). Apollo urges Aeneias to confront him, calling him simply "Peleides Achilles";[4] but Aeneias will not venture forth, as he knows exactly what Peleides Achilles implies: he does not wish to fight against "over-spirited Peleion," nor stand his ground, as he once did, before "swift-footed Achilles."[5] Even as Achilles to him means violent anger, so "swift-footed" means the son of Peleus.[6] His swiftness is an inherited virtue, his anger his own: Aeneias can resist neither.

Aeneias Anchisiades meets divine Achilles.[7] Anchises, who mated with Aphrodite, begot Aeneias; Achilles is divine, an epithet that suggests his genealogy; for at once it is "Peleides" who stands before plain Aeneias; but the son of Peleus, after a simile, becomes Achilles once more,[8] who threatens Aeneias with his power: he speaks to him as divine and as swift-footed, in his lineage and virtue.[9] Aeneias is unimpressed, "great-hearted" as he is,[10] and

1. *Iliad* 20. 1–2, 11. 15–16; 20. 3 = 11. 56.
2. *Ibid.* 20. 45–46, cf. 26–28.
3. Cf. *Iliad* 20. 447.
4. *Iliad* 20. 85.
5. *Ibid.* 20. 88–89, cf. 80.
6. Cf. *Iliad* 22. 188–193.
7. *Iliad* 20. 160.
8. *Ibid.* 20. 164, 174.
9. *Ibid.* 20. 177.
10. *Ibid.* 20. 175.

before launching a recital of his own lineage, calls him Peleides, which he immediately retracts, saying, "*they say* you are the son of Peleus and Thetis, but *I boast* to be the son of Anchises and my mother *is* Aphrodite."[11] The doubt that he raises about Achilles' parentage contrasts with the certainty he has of his own; and yet he puts forward a tedious lineage as a shield against Achilles' superiority, hoping to find in his past a counterweight to Achilles' present greatness.[12]

Aeneias hurls his javelin, Achilles holds up his shield in fear: he fears as "Peleides" the spear of "great-hearted Aeneias," but as soon as he recovers his own spirit and hurls back a spear, he becomes once again Achilles.[13] And as Achilles he rushes at Aeneias shouting dreadfully, but as "Peleides" he would have killed him, had not Poseidon pitied Aeneias and come to where he and "famous Achilles" were standing.[14] He sends down a mist over the eyes of Peleides Achilles, for as the son of his father he would have killed Aeneias, but when Poseidon scatters the mist, he turns into plain Achilles;[15] who speaks to his "great-hearted spirit" and decides to rally the "Danaans lovers of war."[16] Achilles was the first to use *philoptolemoi* ("lovers of war") in speaking of the Myrmidons and Trojans, and only after that do Hector, Lycaon, and Homer employ it: Lycaon when he beseeches Achilles, Homer when he either thinks of Achilles or Achilles is about to speak.[17] It is, like *megathymoi Achaioi*[18] ("high-spirited Achaeans"), an epithet that depends solely on Achilles' presence, or that applies to no one unless they are somehow transformed by Achilles, and become reflections of him.

Hector encourages the "over-spirited Trojans to face "Peleion."[19] Only if he recalls them to their highest excellence, and degrades Achilles to his lowest, patronymic identity, will his rhetoric carry conviction. As the son of his father Achilles can be approached, for "Achilles" he says will not fulfill his boasts, but fail in half of what he promises.[20] Not Peleides Achilles, as it were, with all his excellence, but half of Achilles, the weaker, ancestral half, Hector promises to fight. Apollo, however, disagrees, and reminding Hector of plain Achilles, who is what he thinks he is, forbids him to meet Achilles.[21] Achilles

11. *Ibid.* 20. 200, 206–209, cf. 105–106; 6. 99–100; and Odyssey 1. 215–216, where Telemachus doubts his parentage.
12. Cf. Part II, Chap. I above.
13. *Iliad* 20. 261–263, 273.
14. *Ibid.* 20. 283–291, 320; cf. 302–304.
15. *Ibid.* 20. 321–322, 341–342.
16. *Ibid.* 20. 343, 351–352.
17. *Ibid.* 16. 65, 90, 835; 17. 194, 224; 19. 269; 21. 86; 23. 5, 129.
18. Cf. Part I, Chap. II above.
19. *Iliad* 20. 366.
20. *Ibid.* 20. 367–370; cf. 22. 250–258.
21. *Ibid.* 20. 376–378.

then, shouting dreadfully, engages Ephition, whom he kills and boasts over as "divine."[22] Next he goes after "godlike Polydorus" who "surpassed all the youth in swiftness": Achilles therefore kills him in the capacity of "swift-footed divine Achilles."[23]

Achilles becomes more and more furious: he kills ten heroes one after the other (in thirty-five lines), and yet his name is never mentioned.[24] Here Homer passes judgment on him:[25]

> ou gar ti glycythymos anêr en oud' aganophrôn
> ("for not at all sweet-tempered nor gentle of mood was the man")

He is not "sweet-tempered" but "high-spirited," he is not mild but pitiless. He loses his name in his fury: he is like fire: he is equal to a god.[26] He goes through blood as "high-spirited Achilles," and desires to obtain honor in his father's name.[27]

Achilles continues to destroy the Trojans. He drives them into the river Scamander, and jumps in after them "equal to a god": he is "the Zeus-born" *(ho diogenês),* inhuman and nameless.[28] His name returns: "divine Achilles came on Lycaon as an unforeseen evil."[29] He observes Lycaon as swift-footed and divine, expecting him to flee; but Lycaon stands still, so Achilles, not having to pursue him, drops "swift-footed" and raises his spear to kill him as "divine;"[30] and then Lycaon beseeches him, and Achilles replies "unsweetly" and kills him as plain Achilles.[31]

The river-god Xanthus wishes to stop "divine Achilles,"[32] but the son of Peleus jumps on Asteropaeus, despising his lineage and boasting his own.[33] Asteropaeus is as frightened as Aeneias was: he calls him "high-spirited Peleides."[34] He avoids the spear of Achilles and tries to remove it from the river-bank in which it is lodged: thrice he tries and fails to budge it – the spear of Achilles – but on the fourth try, his last, it is the spear of Aeacides, the spear no one but Achilles could wield.[35] As "Peleides" he slays seven heroes, but as

---

22. *Ibid.* 20. 386–388.
23. *Ibid.* 20. 407–413.
24. *Ibid.* 20. 455–489.
25. *Ibid.* 20. 467; cf. 2. 241; 13. 343–344; 14. 139–140.
26. *Ibid.* 20. 490–494.
27. *Ibid.* 20. 502–503.
28. *Ibid.* 21. 17–18.
29. *Ibid.* 21. 39.
30. *Ibid.* 21. 49, 67.
31. *Ibid.* 21. 98 (cf. 11. 136–137), 116, 120.
32. *Ibid.* 21. 136–138.
33. *Ibid.* 21. 139–199.
34. *Ibid.* 25. 153.
35. *Ibid.* 21. 173–179.

"swift Achilles," by pursuing them, he would have slain more, had not the Xanthus begged him to fight elsewhere.[36] He contemptuously ignores the river, though he pretends he will obey it, and rushes against the Trojans "equal to a god;"[37] but as soon as the Xanthus has reproached Apollo for his neglect of the Trojans, Achilles as "spear-renowned" pursues them.[38] The river, "a great god," swallows up Achilles in its stream, and "Peleides" retreats, and as "swift-footed, divine" he flees.[39] In blaming his mother for his present setback, he looks to heaven as the son of Peleus, and as such Poseidon encourages him.[40]

When Priam looks out over the plain of Troy, he sees "monstrous Peleides."[41] He is afraid lest Achilles jump over the wall, and he calls him that "pernicious, baleful man *(oulos anêr)*.[42] *Oulos* is used of Ares, of fate, and of fire, but nowhere directly of anyone mortal except Achilles.[43] Hector, it is true, is *compared* to a baleful star, or a deadly fire, or a murderous lion *(oulios astêr, oloon pyr leôn oloophrôn)*,[44] but again Achilles really is what Hector only seems to be. He is the end of Hector's ambition. Achilles conditions the use of *oulos,* for in almost half of its instances it is either said by him, or of him, or to him. The formula *epi gêraos oudôi* ("on the threshold of old age"), for example occurs in Homer five times, but only once, when Priam addresses Achilles, does it become *oloôi epi gêraos oudôi,* "the baleful threshold of old age."[45] Priam calls Achilles *oulos anêr,* that anonymous man, and often in the last books he is merely "that man"; *dêios* ("hostile"), *atasthalos* ("ruthless"), *ômêstês* ("savage").[46]

After Homer reveals that the Achaeans would have captured Troy, had not Apollo encouraged Agenor to resist Achilles, Agenor sees him as "Achilles the sacker of cities."[47] Achilles is "sacker of cities" not so much by the cities he has taken,[48] but rather by the Troy he hopes to take. His success has been anticipated in a simile: "As when smoke rises into the broad heavens from a burning city, and the wrath of the gods set it afire, and made toil for all and imposed cares upon many, so Achilles made toil and cares for the Trojans."[49]

36. *Ibid.* 21. 208–213.
37. *Ibid.* 21. 222–227.
38. *Ibid.* 21. 233.
39. *Ibid.* 21. 251, 265.
40. *Ibid.* 21. 272, 288.
41. *Ibid.* 21. 527; 3. 229.
42. *Ibid.* 21. 536.
43. *Ibid.* 24. 39.
44. *Ibid.* 11. 62; 15. 605, 630.
45. *Ibid.* 24. 487.
46. *Ibid.* 20. 467, 21. 314; 22. 38, 84, 418; 24. 207 (cf. 82), 212, 506, 520.
47. *Ibid.* 21. 544–550.
48. *Ibid.* 9. 328.

Achilles is the smoke, which foretells the end of Troy, even as he is like the wrath of the gods (who now look down on the scene) that sets the torch to Troy.[50] If we look back over the similes of Achilles, this one belongs to them as the last in a series. He was, at the beginning of his exploits, first like Ares and then like a lion, his divine and natural aspects alternately displayed; and again he became like a god, but instead of returning to an animal identity, he foreshadowed Hephaestus' help and seemed equal to fire; after which he once more was a god and fire (they now coalesced); and again he became like a god but then returned to the animal world in the shape of a dolphin, for he plunges into the Scamander to pursue the Trojans; afterwards he was a god and an eagle as he fled the river, and again the Scamander itself compared him to the gods, while as soon as the river subsided, he reunited fire with divinity, resembling both the smoke of a city and the wrath of the gods.[51] As Achilles conquers Troy in a simile, so the gods dispute later "about Hector the corpse and Achilles the sacker of cities,"[52] for Hector alone made the city stand, and after his death the Trojans weep as if "all Ilium were already smouldering."[53] Although Achilles, by killing Hector, becomes *ptoliporthos* ("waster of cities"), it is nothing but poetic license that grants it, which leaves him as ineffective in action as he was before in his absence.

We have traced the action and the epithets of Achilles up to his encounter with Hector, trying to show how in these last books the epithets become more striking, exact, and horrible, while his conventional epithets tend to diminish; how the anonymity of Achilles is stressed more and more, until his patronymic almost disappears in the end;[54] how, in short, he has prepared himself for his battle with Hector.

---

49. *Ibid.* 21. 522–525; cf. 18. 207–214.
50. *Mênis* ("wrath") is used only of Achilles *(Iliad* 1. 1; 9. 517; 19. 35, 75) or the gods (1.75; 5. 34, 178, 444; 13. 624; 15. 122; 16. 711; 21. 523).
51. *Iliad* 20. 46, 164–175, 447, 490–494; 21. 12–14, 18, 22–24, 227, 252 –254, 315.
52. *Ibid.* 24. 108.
53. *Ibid.* 22.410–411, cf. 383–384; 6. 403; 24. 499.
54. The frequency of his patronymic is: 20 in Book 20, 12 in Book 21, 11 in Book 22, 17 in Book 23, 5 in Book 24.

Chapter VIII
Achilles and Hector

Hector is a civil Achilles. Respect for those weaker than himself dominates everything he does. His mother and father cannot persuade him to avoid Achilles, ashamed, as he is, lest someone baser than himself might say, "Hector, trusting to his strength, destroyed his people."[1] He is like Menelaus who, when he saw Hector advancing towards him, wished to flee but feared the reproach of the Achaeans, if he should abandon Patroclus who died for his honor.[2] If Menelaus had resisted singly the Trojans, he would have done so out of shame, but, unlike Hector, he reasoned it away, thinking that no one could blame him, were he unwilling to fight against a god-favored man. Hector is held by shame. He fears more keenly the scorn of Troy's citizens than Menelaus the scorn of the camp. His fear of others, not any inner restraint, makes Hector stand up to Achilles.[3] He had given to Andromache, when she foreboded his death, two reasons why he must continue to fight: his shame and his spirit.[4] Even as now he felt shame then, but his high spirit, which had been trained to be brave, no longer is present. He is forced on by a necessity as great as Achilles' that has nothing to do with virtue. He hoped to kill Ajax and thus acquire immortal fame: now he is content to die famously before Troy.[5] He is concerned more with his own renown than with the fate of his people: his sense of shame has placed him above shame, and made him disregard any interest but his own. Although he cares more for Andromache than for the rest of Troy, he prefers to act rashly than to save even her;[6] for to maintain his own self-esteem exceeds all other cares. In this respect he resembles Achilles, who had cherished his anger, though it meant death to the Achaeans, and now belatedly defends them for the sake of Patroclus.

Hector to Andromache was everything: father and mother, brother and husband.[7] Achilles was everything to Patroclus: he compared himself to a

1. *Iliad* 22. 105–107.
2. *Ibid.* 17. 91–105.
3. Cf. *Iliad* 11. 404–410; Schadewaldt *op. cit.,* pp. 61–62.
4. *Iliad* 6. 441–446.
5. *Ibid.* 22. 108–110, cf. 514.
6. *Ibid.* 6. 450–465.
7. *Ibid.* 6. 429–430.

mother and Patroclus to his daughter; he will be compared to a father who burns the bones of his son; and Apollo will be indignant that he shows more care for Patroclus than men do for a brother.[8] And yet in spite of their responsibilities, both Hector and Achilles shirk them. Hector has become an alien because of his shame, Achilles was isolated from the Achaeans out of shamelessness.[9] Both are driven to a combat each had sought to avoid. Achilles' vain effort to re-establish his honor corresponds to Hector's attempt to correct his mistake: as if Achilles could balance the death of Hector against the loss of Patroclus, and Hector, in clinging to his civil shame, could maintain his renown. At the cost of Troy's fall he preserves his shame. He abandons Troy. And Achilles, in reacquiring his martial spirit, loses his virtue. Each has made his own excellence contradict itself. In his desire to be the perfect hero, each has ceased to be a hero at all.

Hector wonders if he could escape Achilles' fury, were he to offer him the return of Helen and all the wealth Paris had taken with her; but he cuts himself short in so idle a hope by saying, "There is no time now to chatter with him from oak and from rock, like a youth and a maid, as a youth and a maid chat with one another."[10] To while away the time (so neatly expressed in the epanalepsis) a youth and a maid may beguile each other with their talk of fabulous origins and "old stories":[11] but Hector must resolve his dispute with Achilles as quickly as possible,[12] and were he to offer Helen back, who was the *archê* and origin of the war,[13] he would be guilty of a gross anachronism. Patroclus' death is the cause of Achilles' reappearance, while Helen's bigamy has become as mythical as a lineage from oak and from rock. The desire for immortal fame had already discarded Helen, and though that desire is by now less vehement, she does not reassume her former role. She has been replaced by Patroclus. An obsolete Helen cannot appease a revengeful Achilles, not even if he himself pretends that he fights in a foreign land for her sake.[14] She had been unsuccessful in settling the war, when the certainty of Troy's capture inspired the Achaeans;[15] and she is no more successful now, as Achilles seeks his revenge for him who can never be restored.

Achilles pursues Hector round the walls of Troy, and though he is swift-footed, he cannot overtake him: "As in a dream one cannot pursue him who

8. *Ibid.* 16. 7–11; 23. 222–225; 24. 46–48; cf. 9. 632–633.
9. *Ibid.* 22. 123–125.
10. *Ibid.* 22. 126–128.
11. Cf. *Odyssey* 19. 162–163; A. B. Cooke, *CR,* xv, 1901, p. 326; U. Wilamowitz, *op. cit.,* pp. 97–98; P. von der Muehl, *op. cit.,* p. 234, who translates Hesiod *Theogony* 35 as *"alte Geschichten."*
12. *Iliad* 22. 129–130.
13. *Ibid.* 22. 116.
14. *Ibid.* 19. 324–325.
15. *Ibid.* 7. 400–402.

flees, and neither is one able to elude nor the other to pursue, so Achilles was unable to catch Hector nor Hector to escape."[16] They belong to a dream's endless pursuit, where the pursuer cannot catch the pursued, nor the pursued escape the pursuer. Achilles' swiftness, which his epithet *podôkês* ("swift-footed") had promised, is in the act belied. He does not measure up to his notices. His most outstanding virtue, by which he excelled Ajax (his closest rival in perfection), is put to the test and found wanting. And Hector, who thought that his encounter with Achilles would be more decisive than the dalliance of a youth and a maid, prolongs it as long as he can. Just as they make a circuit of the wall three times, so in their shared dream they thrice cannot elude one another. But the dream is more real than their combat, for Hector's death is supernatural. Were it not that Apollo deserts him and Athena deceives him, Hector would have continued to outdistance Achilles. His death is contrived. It satisfies Achilles' revenge, it bolsters his prestige, it puts together out of the scraps of his virtue a final victory. He does not prove himself superior to Hector, but only proves that the gods surpass both. What was to demonstrate his excellence merely shows up his weakness. Patroclus' death was necessary for Achilles to realize his guilt; Hector's death is necessary to make a fitting end. Homer ennobles Achilles as much as he can, and after his real death in the eighteenth book, allows this armored shell to become human again.

When Hector asks Achilles to respect his corpse, even as he would give back Achilles' were he to die, Achilles savagely replies: "As there can be no trusted oaths between lions and men, nor are wolves and sheep of one heart in their spirit, but ever think evil of one another, so you and I cannot be friends."[17] Heroes had often been compared to either lions and wolves, or men and sheep: but it had always been a momentary likeness and not a permanent condition. The similes had been the comments of Homer, and not what the heroes thought of themselves. The accidental difference between man and man had been expressed by the natural antagonisms among animals: but it had never been elevated to a rule. Achilles is quite willing to let Hector be a man, and assume for himself the role of a lion.[18] He does not intend it as a chance identity, but as nicely expressive of his lasting hatred. He wishes that his fury and strength would allow him to devour Hector,[19] as if a simile to him were but an optative, and to be a beast his ultimate ambition.

Hector at his death wears the arms of Achilles,[20] which Patroclus had worn to deceive the Trojans, so that they would mistake himself for Achilles;[21]

16. *Ibid.* 22. 199–201.
17. *Ibid.* 22. 262–265.
18. Cf. *Iliad* 12. 167–172; 17. 20–23.
19. *Iliad* 22. 346–347; cf. 25. 22–24; 24. 41–44.
20. *Ibid.* 17. 183–197.

and they were tricked enough to grant the Achaeans a short respite, while they themselves were forced back to the city.[22] Hector, then, in wearing these arms, partly resembles Achilles.[23] He resembles him as much as Patroclus ever did. He faces Achilles in the guise of Patroclus, who, as the image of Achilles, had gone to war, and now returns to confront him as Hector. Hector is what Patroclus had seemed to be before his death: a mere extension of Achilles. As Patroclus' death made him an individual and not just a lesser Achilles, so the death of Hector stresses the difference between arms and the man. He must be killed where Achilles' armor does not cover him: where the quickest death for a man happens to be:[24] where Achilles can see most clearly his own flaw. Hector is almost *panchalkeos* ("all made of bronze"),[25] almost a thing, almost Achilles. He shares with Achilles the murder of Patroclus, and with Patroclus a likeness to Achilles. Thus Patroclus is the means to the final identity of Achilles and Hector.

21.   *Ibid.* 11. 798–801 = 16. 40–43.
22.   *Ibid.* 16. 278–282.
23.   Cf. *Iliad* 17. 214 v. i. *megathymôi Pêleiôni* ("[like] to high-spirited Peleides").
24.   *Iliad* 22. 322–325; cf. 8. 324–326.
25.   Cf. *Iliad* 20. 102; cf. Eustathius *ad loc.,* 4. 510–511; 13. 321–323.

Chapter IX
The Funeral Games

After the death of Hector, Achilles triumphantly ends his speech with a paean, which includes all the Achaeans in his own success: "We have slain divine Hector, whom the Trojans prayed to as a god."[1] Although he slew Hector by himself (if we omit Athena's assistance),[2] and had forbidden anyone else to attack Hector, lest he might come second in the kill,[3] he feels for an instant no longer isolated, and is quite willing to share his greatness with the other Achaeans. If he can only be numbered among them, they may take part credit in his victory. His slaughter of Trojans has restored his generosity and given him once more a good opinion of himself. He so far forgets his grief in the display of his prowess, that he wants to press his advantage,[4] as if he had resumed the war to gratify the Achaeans, and not to avenge Patroclus' death. The war almost regains its lost purpose – the destruction of Troy – and Patroclus almost becomes as superfluous as Helen – nothing but an irritant to immortal fame – until Achilles checks himself and remembers his guilt, "unwept, unburied Patroclus."[5] He cannot shake off Patroclus as the Achaeans ignored Helen, nor can Patroclus be converted as Helen was into some higher end. He must always remain a private sorrow. Achilles must cling to Patroclus as to himself; he can no more abandon him than himself; he must always remember the crime he has done. Torn between his reacquired virtue and his festering guilt, he cannot quite hold on to his new status, nor slough off completely his former isolation. As he has been galvanized into action by the death of Patroclus, he must keep himself alive by continuous performance. To make amends to Patroclus, he abuses Hector,[6] for it is the only action he can do that does not betray Patroclus (by starting a spiral of ever-greater aggrandizement); but the longer he prolongs this mechanical savagery, the more withdrawn he becomes, and, instead of allaying his guilt, he only increases his remorse.

1. *Iliad* 22. 393–394; cf. 16. 243–244.
2. Cf. 22. 216–223.
3. *Iliad* 22. 205–207; cf. 16. 87–90.
4. *Ibid.* 22. 379–384.
5. *Ibid.* 22. 385–387; cf. 9. 608–610.
6. *Ibid.* 22. 395–404.

Weariness at last overcomes Achilles, and he falls asleep on the shore, only to be awakened by the ghost of Patroclus, who complains that he now neglects and has forgotten him.[7] Achilles then, promising Patroclus to bury his bones with his own, stretches out his hand to embrace him; but Patroclus like smoke eludes his grasp, and Achilles, astonished as by a revelation, cries out:[8]

> ô popoi ê ra ti esti kai ein Aidao domoisi
> psychê kai eidôlon, atar phrenes ouk eni tampan
> Alas! Even in the house of Hades the soul and image are something, but there are not at all *phrenes*.

The *psychê* is something after death, but there are no *phrenes* at all.[9] Death is the loss of *phrenes:* the powerlessness to fulfill what one desires. Patroclus cannot clasp Achilles' hand, for though his ghost looks exactly like his living self (in height and in features, in voice and in clothes),[10] he can only gibber and vanish like smoke. Yet his failure is no different from Achilles', who cannot abuse Hector's corpse. He threatens to give Hector to the dogs, but Aphrodite protects him, anointed with ambrosial oil, and Apollo covers him with a cloud, lest the sun dry him.[11] No matter how much Achilles tries to humiliate Hector, he only succeeds in humiliating himself. He is as ineffectual as the dead Patroclus and as paralyzed now in his action as he was before when he refused to fight. He had thought that it was his *psychê* that he risked whenever he went into battle – *aiei emên psychên paraballomenos polemizein* ("always risking my *psychê* in fighting"),[12] but now he knows his *psychê* would have survived his death, while his *phrenes* have disappeared in his ineffectiveness.[13]

Achilles tries to burn Patroclus, but the pyre will not light; and though he prays to Boreas and Zephyrus and promises them sacrifices, they do not hear him. Iris must go in person to the winds, begging them to heed Achilles' summons, and only then do they came and fan to a blaze the pyre.[14] What should happen as a matter of course must now happen by the gods. Achilles cannot even start a fire without divine intervention. He has become so isolated from the ordinary world that only the gods can keep him going. The Trojans have no trouble in burning Hector; but Patroclus' death, having broken Achilles'

7.   *Ibid.* 23.59–70.
8.   *Ibid.* 23. 103–104.
9.   Cf. *Odyssey* 10. 493; 11. 475–476.
10.   *Iliad* 23. 66–67; cf. 2. 57–58.
11.   *Ibid.* 23. 184–191.
12.   *Ibid.* 9. 322.
13.   Cf. *Iliad* 14. 139–142.
14.   *Iliad* 23. 192–216.

last tie with man, brings about his break with the world. He is a breach in the world. He belongs now completely to another region where every action must be managed by the gods. If the winds had answered his appeal by themselves, if Iris did not have to plead for him, the scene would have shown Achilles' hold over them. But they do not respond; they are indifferent, as Iris is not, to his grief. The isolation of Achilles is in this chain of command; he cannot start a fire directly, nor can he enlist the winds in his cause; Iris must intervene. Even as the gods gave him ambrosia and nectar, so that he could demonstrate his virtue, so now the winds must sustain his simplest desire. They are like the knocking at the gate in *Macbeth*: they serve to recall the humdrum world, from which we, in our sympathy with Achilles, have been slowly removed. The winds seem rather comical, as they sit at their feast; but it is we, who have fasted with Achilles and seen the world through his eyes, that have become tragic. We have come to expect failure: that the corpse of Hector should not decompose, and that fire should not burn. Cause and effect, will and act, have been split apart, and only the gods hold them together.

When the pyre has been quenched and the bones of Patroclus collected, Achilles sets up a series of games in honor of Patroclus; but Achilles himself does not participate. He stands apart and distributes prizes. He says his horses are the best, but he cannot prove it.[15] He says he would take the first prize, if he competed; but he cannot put his boast to the test. He is the swiftest of heroes, but he could not overtake Hector, nor can he now excel Odysseus and Oilean Ajax. His virtues are as idle now as they were at the beginning. They hold a promise that is never fulfilled. He obtains the epithet "swift-footed" more often in this book, when he can do nothing with it, than anywhere else.[16] Only here is he called "hero,"[17] and his patronymic, which had tended to disappear during his exploits, again becomes frequent, for he regains somewhat his former honor. He sees reviewed before him all of the virtues he himself once had, just as he saw in the catalogue of ships all the glory he squandered. Homer had listed him in the catalogue, even though he played there no role; and he assigns him here the task of offering prizes to others, since he cannot win a prize for himself. He is no more a part of the games than he was a member of Agamemnon's host. He is as isolated at the end as he was at the start; there by the paralysis of anger, here by the paralysis of guilt. Though his authority has never been greater, all his power is gone. He has reversed roles with Agamemnon, whose power he now acknowledges and whose authority is now his own. He gives Agamemnon the first prize, without proof, in the casting of the spear. "We know how much you excel us all and are the best in

15. *Ibid.* 23. 274–284.
16. The frequency of "swift-footed" is: 6 in Book 20, 5 in Book 21, 6 in Book 22, 14 in Book 23, 4 in Book 24.
17. *Iliad* 23. 824, 896.

power and in spear."[18] Achilles had insisted before that he was the best, and that Agamemnon had only usurped that title;[19] but now he piously grants Agamemnon more than we ourselves would admit. As Agamemnon is best in the catalogue,[20] so is he best in the games; and as it was the fiat of Homer and of Zeus that made him there outstanding, so it is the fiat of Achilles here that lends him prestige. Not only does Achilles abandon all his pretensions to rule, but he leans over backwards to enhance Agamemnon. He heaps upon him all of his own ambitions and makes him as powerful and as absolute as he himself once was. And yet, in not letting Agamemnon prove himself, he hints at his real weakness and his own generosity.

Among the games Achilles set up was discus-throwing, and the discus itself was the prize, a mass of iron which he had taken from the sacred city of Eetion.[21] There would be nothing remarkable in this, if we did not remember the other objects that came from there: the blameless horse Pedasus, the lyre with which Achilles pleased his heart, Hector's wife Andromache, and the concubine of Agamemnon, Cryseis.[22] The return of Cryseis provoked Agamemnon and led to his taking Briseis, who came from Lyrnessus near Thebe (the city of Eetion);[23] Andromache, the wife of his enemy, stood for Patroclus in the story of Phoenix; the lyre showed up Achilles' inaction and the wasting of his virtue;[24] the death of Pedasus, as that of Patroclus, was the death of the mortal Achilles;[25] and the mass of iron, which he may not toss, stresses again Achilles' idleness. Thus the city of Eetion is Achilles' city of failure. On that expedition which showed Achilles at his best, he captured the implements that now reveal his defects. He must even in war, while he proves himself virtuous, collect the symbols of his future doom. He is never apart from his destiny: the seeds of his wrath, his isolation, and his guilt were contained in the evidence of his prowess. His casual acquisitions, which were the spoils of war, instigate his wrath (Chryseis and Briseis), recall his unpracticed virtue (the lyre and the discus), and destroy his humanity (Pedasus and Andromache). What should have confirmed his excellence signify instead his tragedy.

18. *Ibid.* 23. 890–891.
19. Cf. Part I, Chap. III, IV, above.
20. *Iliad* 2. 482–483, 579–580.
21. *Ibid.* 23. 826–828.
22. *Ibid.* 1. 366–369; 6. 395–397; 9. 188; 16. 153.
23. *Ibid.* 2. 689–691.
24. Cf. Part II, Chap. III above.
25. Cf. Part II, Chap. V above.

Chapter X
Achilles and Priam

Achilles cannot sleep after the funeral games, where he has seen every kind of excellence that was once his own boast, and he remembers Patroclus, "for whose manhood and strength he longs."[1] The loss he sustained in the death of Patroclus is made more poignant by the "manhood and strength" that the other Achaeans have just displayed, who mock Achilles' present ineffectiveness, since he has only the memory of his past actions to measure against them. Unlike Odysseus who gladly forgets his toil as he sails homeward, Achilles must now regret that all his bravery is over.[2] His self-inflicted grief does not allow him respite: he must always go over again the irrevocable past. As the recalling of what he was is its empty iteration, so his dragging of Hector's corpse is vainly repeated, for he can no more restore Patroclus by his memory, than he can disgrace Hector by dragging.[3] Apollo protects Hector even as Aphrodite had before, and since they keep him beautiful, they deprive Achilles of everything but the semblance of action.

All the gods who favor the Trojans pity Hector, and urge Hermes to steal his corpse; but Hera, Athena, and Poseidon object because of their old hatred of Troy.[4] No longer are Achilles and Hector central, but the war has become once again a mere feud among the gods. The wrath of Achilles was an interlude in the Trojan war: it suspended its first cause – Paris and Helen – and allowed the heroes a greater scope to their ambitions; but now that Achilles has almost worked out his tragedy, the war returns to its origins. He has become as superfluous as Helen once was. Yet Homer makes this heavenly dispute his own final indictment of Achilles. Were Hermes to steal Hector's corpse, Achilles would never become human. He would be left to rot in his savage isolation, without ever understanding his dependence on the gods and other men. He would have been like Sophocles' Ajax, had not Athena intervened and saved him from himself; for it is she who in diverting his fury away from the Atreidae, makes him realize the enormity of his crime. If Ajax had killed them, he would never have killed himself, and thus asserted his claim

1. *Iliad* 24. 6.
2. *Iliad* 24. 8–9; *Odyssey* 13. 91–92; cf. *Iliad* 19. 319–321; 23. 56; *Odyssey* 7. 215–221.
3. *Iliad* 24. 9–21; cf. 490–492.
4. *Ibid.* 24. 22–30.

to greatness. He would have rejoiced in the slaughter, as we see him doing, and he would have been killed by the Achaeans, without reacquiring the honour he deserves. Suicide is the one reflective action of Ajax which shows us his virtue stripped of rewards. So Achilles, were Hector to disappear like Paris, would never be forced to give him back to Priam, by which show of maganimity he is admitted into the family of men. To feel shame once again, to pity someone weaker than himself, redeems Achilles, so that he can eat, sleep, and even lie down beside Briseis.[5]

Although Ajax obtained a posthumous triumph by his own hand, and Achilles is truly noble as he confronts Priam, yet we must never forget that Athena alone made Ajax' suicide possible, and that Zeus alone brought about Achilles' vindication. That they both follow the prompting of the gods, when they could have resisted, is at once a proof of their greatness and of their insufficiency. The gods make the heroic world inhabitable. Had they not stopped Achilles, he would have continued his senseless dragging of Hector. He would never have escaped from his monstrous impotence. Had Hera prevailed, and her distinction between Hector and Achilles been accepted (that a mortal is less than the offspring of a god),[6] Achilles would never have realized his own humanity. Achilles is as mortal as Hector, and his divine parentage allows him no more irresponsibility toward men than a mortal parentage allows Hector to betray Troy. If Hector's excess of shame, in putting his own renown before Troy's safety, destroyed him, so Achilles is no different by his lack of shame, which also destroys him. Achilles' honor might be more than Hector's,[7] but his fate is the same. If Hector only seemed to be the son of a god,[8] while Achilles is half-divine, yet they both share a common death. If two men equally desire immortality, but one has the edge in the means to obtain it, he still is no different from the other. As long as the gap between the gods and men remains open (and if they are to be distinguished, it must be so), no matter how similar to them a man may seem, the distinction is fatal. Hector's funeral can end the *Iliad,* and the scene be a purely Trojan affair, since the difference between a divine and a mortal lineage, like that between Achaean and Trojan, has at last disappeared. In losing his divine status and in gaining a civil shame, Achilles becomes the image of Hector, whose funeral can represent his own.

Priam decides to reclaim his son, after Iris has urged him in the name of Zeus, and his friends escort him as far as the plain, "with great lamentations, as if he were going to his death."[9] Zeus then sends Hermes to conduct him to Achilles' ships, so that no one might see him, "before he comes to Peleion."

5.   *Ibid.* 24. 675–676.
6.   *Ibid.* 24. 56–63.
7.   *Ibid.* 24. 66.
8.   *Ibid.* 24. 258–259.
9.   *Ibid.* 24. 322–328.

If we remember that Hermes is the conductor of the dead,[10] it is not strange that he should be Priam's guide. Achilles died when he heard of Patroclus' death, and was miraculously revived in order to have his revenge;[11] but now that he has finished his work, he belongs once again to Hades.[12] With the coming of night, Hermes leads Priam to Hades, where a ghostly Achilles was as unable to harm Hector as Sisyphus to roll his stone up the hill. His paralysis is the price of his guilt, which he cannot expiate no matter how long he may weep. His every action is timeless, for it has no end. What he says of grief, that there is no effect nor action in it,[13] is equally true of his guilt, which holds him in Hades, where causes have no consequence and desires lack fulfillment. "For how long do you devour your heart," Thetis asked her son, who, in abandoning his wish to devour Hector, has turned upon himself.[14] He becomes his sole object. He no longer has anything beyond himself, on which he can vent his fury, but must always be reminded, and yet remain always unsated, by the past – the bones of Patroclus and the body of Hector. His grief alternates with his guilt, abusing Hector or devouring himself. He can never escape from his own hell.

In order to stress the unreality that surrounds Achilles, Homer makes as real as possible the scenes at Troy. He reports all the speeches at Troy – what Iris said to Priam, what Priam to Hecuba and Hecuba to him – while he makes Achilles in two lines agree to return Hector's corpse; and though "mother and son in the throng of ships spoke many winged words to one another," we do not know what they said.[15] This silence conveys more effectively than his words could have done the isolation of Achilles. It allows us to imagine the magnitude of his grief and prevents us from underestimating it. Its vagueness makes it more precise. At Troy, however, Homer minutely describes how they harnessed a wagon to bring Hector back; and if, for all its exactness, it has never yet been fully explained,[16] at least it stamps Priam's setting forth as vivid and real, so that the tent of Achilles, which has as many rooms as a palace, may seem the more insubstantial. Its huge doors, which require three men to open and three to close, do not belong to the same world as that of this

10. *Odyssey* 24. 14.
11. Cf. Part II, Chap. VI above.
12. That the suffix *-de* (denoting motion toward, cf. English "-wards") is only used here of a person – *Pêleiônade*, "the-son-of-Peleus-wards" (*Iliad* 24. 338: it is unique until Ap. Rhod. iii. 647) – recalling at once *thanatonde*, "deathwards" above and the common *Aïdosde* "towards [the house of Hades" (24. 328; cf. 9. 158, 312–313), also suggests this. Cf. Horace C i. x. 13-20. Note too the unique locative *Aïdi*, "in Hades," at 23. 244 in Achilles' mouth.
13. *Iliad* 24. 524; *Odyssey* 10. 202, 568.
14. *Iliad* 24. 128–129; 22. 346–347.
15. *Ibid.* 24. 139–142.
16. *Ibid.* 24. 266–274; cf. Leaf II, App. M, pp. 623–629.

wagon;[17] for it reflects the loneliness of Achilles' guilt and the vastness of his grief, and has nothing to do with the everyday world, but corresponds to the fantasy he himself has made.

As soon as Priam entered Achilles' tent, "he grasped his knees and kissed his dread man-slaying hands, which had killed many of his sons: as when a great doom seizes a man, so that he kills another in his fatherland, and comes to a foreign land, to the home of a rich man, and wonder holds those who see him, so Achilles was astonished beholding godlike Priam."[18] The simile seems pointless except for the wonder felt at the coming of a murderer: for Priam did not kill anyone, but Achilles, with his "man-slaying hands," did slay Priam's sons. If Achilles had come to Priam, it would have been more natural to compare him thus than to compare the innocent Priam to a murderer, and the guilty Achilles to a wealthy man. Priam seems to represent someone else, and I would suggest he is the dead Patroclus, who once came to Peleus, having killed his playmate in Opoeis.[19] Priam would come then in the guise of Patroclus to Achilles, who would now be Peleus; for just as Peleus "kindly" received Patroclus, so Zeus promised that Achilles would kindly receive Priam.[20] We are transported back to Phthia, to the palace of rich Peleus, so that the courtyard, megaron, hall and antechamber are all, metaphorically, in place.[21] If Achilles is cut off from the present, Priam must appeal to the past. He must conjure up a civil world, where Achilles would feel again the sense of shame: so his first words are, "Remember your father."[22] If Achilles remembers his father, he will acknowledge the mortal half of himself; he will remember Peleus' reception of Patroclus and will thus pity Priam: "Achilles wept for his father and in turn for Patroclus."[23] By this shift in identities, Achilles becomes civil. He weeps for Peleus, for that is himself; he weeps for Patroclus, for that is Priam. Achilles confronts Patroclus, no longer as a ghost but as the father of his enemy, who asks him for the corpse of him who killed him. But Achilles killed Patroclus as much as Hector did: thus Priam as Patroclus asks for Achilles. The corpse of Hector is mortal Achilles, and it is he as well as Hector who is buried at Troy.[24] *Quis utrumque recte norit, ambos noverit* ("'Whoever knows either rightly knows both'").

17. *Ibid.* 24. 448–456.
18. *Ibid.* 24. 477–483.
19. *Ibid.* 23. 85–90.
20. *Ibid.* 23. 90; 24. 158.
21. *Ibid.* 24. 452, 644–647, 673–674.
22. *Ibid.* 24. 486.
23. *Ibid.* 24. 511–512.
24. Cf. *Iliad* 20. 127–128 with 24. 209–210; 16. 852–853 with 24. 131–132.

Epilogue

Homer began his *Iliad* by asking the Muse to sing the wrath of Achilles; he asked her to describe not Achilles but Achilles'.wrath, which began at a certain moment and brought about a certain end. We hardly see Achilles apart from his wrath, and though he may exist apart, he would not then be a subject for poetry. Achilles is as unintelligible without his wrath as he is inconceivable away from Troy. Achilles is his wrath, and his wrath is his fate. It is his greatness. The moment of the *Iliad* is all of Achilles. This single blaze is he. He has no history. Were we to see him sacking the city of Eetion, we might mistake him for someone else. As a mixture of all the heroes – the pride of Agamemnon and the ancestral virtue of Diomedes, the loyalty of Patroclus and the shame of Menelaus, the power of Ajax and the swiftness of his namesake, the beauty of Paris and the greatness of Hector – Achilles does not assert his independence until he retires from the war. Not until he is alone, does he show himself unique. He only becomes visible when he is about to die. Nothing much can be said about him that does not concern his death. The last days of Achilles tell us what he always was, for only in departing from heroic virtue, and in assuming an unheroic posture, does he reveal himself.

When we turn to the *Odyssey,* we find Homer indifferent to what stories the Muse might sing: "At any point, goddess, daughter of Zeus, begin to tell even us."[1] If the Muse had begun differently, and described Odysseus' other adventures, we would have seen the same man. There is no single adventure that makes Odysseus unique. Whether he slays the suitors or blinds Polyphemus, Odysseus cannot be taken for someone else. If he had never gone to Hades, he would still be a subject for poetry. Homer must select from Odysseus' travels those that would form a poetic unity; but that unity lies outside himself and is more imposed upon him than dictated by him. Teiresias tells him how he will die,[2] but that death does not tell us more what kind of a man he is than the episodes Homer chose. His fate is not all of himself as it is for Achilles; it would not reveal anything more. He is *polutropos,* "of many turns."

The Achilles of Homer and Achilles himself coincide. There is no non-Homeric Achilles; but there would be an Odysseus without Homer. Odysseus

1. *Odyssey* 1. 10.
2. *Ibid.* 11. 134–136.

partly tells his own story, and for a single night among the Phaeacians he usurps Homer's role. He is both different from and the same as Homer; but Achilles, as it were, employs Homer and lets him be his chronicler. He is the doer, Homer the talker, and had Homer sung of another man, Achilles would not have survived at all. Except for one fatal instance, Achilles does not bother about his fame.[3] Odysseus, however, sings his own praise and does not need Homer's muse. He is more independent than Achilles: he stands apart from his poem. He is not completely contrived. It is the nature of the tragic hero to be inseparable from his poet, while the comic hero exists even away from his fictitious self. What would Ajax be without Sophocles? a bad loser. Would Socrates be different in life? Achilles is poetic: he cannot be translated into the common world. He can only breathe in the world that Homer made for him: in the *Odyssey* he is a ghost in Hades.

The tragic hero has character, the comic hero personality. The one is stamped with certain attributes and cast into a single mold; the other wears as many masks as he needs. The comic hero can lie; the tragic hero must tell what he thinks is the truth.[4] He does not shift from one scene to the next, but he always carries with him all of himself. He cannot suppress nor conceal. He can never be a hypocrite. He is sublimely unaware of chance: he would not stoop to craft. Although Achilles is a work of art, he would not use art himself. He could no more tell Polyphemus that his name is "No-one" than restrain himself from killing him. The tragic hero is forever trapped in the Cyclops' cave. To deceive another is to deceive himself; he would never sidestep an approaching doom. He himself weaves the net that ensnares him, for he feels that only necessity can prove his greatness. His imprudence is his foresight. It springs the trap of his fate, and in his fate he lives. He fosters and feeds the extreme situation, so that, with the odds all against him, he can make his killing. The comic hero, however, is a catalyst: there are no "solutions" that can precipitate his compound self: he is personally inert though he may disturb everyone else; but the tragic hero enters into an "irreversible reaction," and "there's an end." After a certain point he cannot retreat but must always advance to his end. There are no rehearsals for the great event. He can never repeat his past. Achilles made his way into his death, Odysseus talked his way out of his. Odysseus finds dangers, Achilles invents them. Poseidon prevented Odysseus' return home, and Odysseus, no matter how much he might have profited from his travels, did not welcome them. Achilles becomes angry at Agamemnon: no prophecy foretold it. He worked out for himself how he was going to die. Odysseus' death is divorced from him. Achilles made his fate his own affair; he set the stage for the end. He is, in sense, the real poet of the *Iliad,* and Homer nothing but his scribe.

3.   Cf. Part II, Chap. III above.
4.   Cf. Plato *Hippias Minor* 364d7–365d4, 369a7–371e5.

The tragic hero is rebellious, the comic hero revolutionary. Whatever laws the one may break seem to himself undeliberated acts, while to the other every violation is a matter of policy. One follows a destiny, the other a program. Achilles and Coriolanus invite disaster; they do not play it. Odysseus and Prospero calculate each move: they leave nothing to chance. To be rebellious is to pit nobility against necessity; to be revolutionary is to match wits with chance. There is no victory in rebellion: there is only the deed itself. The tragic hero "kicks against the pricks," though he knows what Hector means,

> *xunos Enualios, kai te ktaneonta katekta*
> Alike to all is the God of War, and he slays utterly even him who would slay.

Note

There are at least two related errors in this study. Under the impression that Homer had to be proved a poet through the smallest element, I attempted to vindicate the epithets rather than to look at the larger units of action, which, however traditional their parts may be, could not be subject to tradition in the same way. In my "The *Aristeia* of Diomedes and the Plot of the *Iliad*" I tried to make up for this defect. And again under the influence of modern poetry, I believed that the discernment of a symbolic pattern was enough to show the poet's hand, even though the pattern could not be grounded in any plausible sequence of actions. So I thought it was not necessary to link Achilles' rebellion in Book I with the combat between Paris and Menelaus in Book III. That combat merely signified the state of affairs at Troy prior to the shift to the love of fame away from the original cause of the war, the love of Helen. I did not observe that Menelaus' acceptance of Paris' challenge meant that Menelaus no longer claimed Helen by law but saw the necessity to prove his claim. Though Achilles failed to replace Agamemnon, he forced everyone to acknowledge the right of natural right. By reading Homer too poetically I did not read him poetically enough.

Selected Works by Seth Benardete

"The Daimonion of Socrates: A Study of Plato's *Theages*." Master's thesis. University of Chicago, 1953.

"Achilles and Hector: The Homeric Hero." Ph.D. dissertation. University of Chicago, 1955. Published in *St. John's Review* in two parts: Spring 1985: 31–58; Summer 1985: 85–114.

Aeschylus, *Suppliant Maidens and Persians*. Translation. Chicago: University of Chicago Press, 1957.

"Plato *Sophist* 231b1–7." *Phronesis* 5, no. 3 (1960): 129–139.

"Vat. Gr. 2181: An Unknown Aristophanes MS." *Harvard Studies in Classical Philology* (1962): 241–48.

"Achilles and the *Iliad*." *Hermes* 91, no. 1 (1963): 1–16. Reprinted in *The Argument of the Action: Essays on Greek Poetry and Philosophy* by Seth Benardete, edited by Ronna Burger and Michael Davis. Chicago: University of Chicago Press, 2000.

"The Right, the True, and the Beautiful." *Glotta* 41, nos. 1–2 (1963): 54–62. "*Eidos* and *Diaersis* in Plato's *Statesman*." *Philologus* 107, nos. 3–4 (1963): 193–226.

"Some Misquotations of Homer in Plato." *Phronesis* 8, no. 2 (1963): 173–178.

"The Crimes and Arts of Prometheus." *Rheinisches Museum für Philologie* 107, no. 2 (1964): 126–139.

"Sophocles' *Oedipus Tyrannus*." In *Ancients and Moderns*, edited by Joseph Cropsey, 1–15. New York: Basic Books, 1964. Reprinted in *Sophocles: Twentieth Century Views*, edited by Thomas Woodard. Englewood Cliffs, NJ.: Prentice Hall, 1966. Reprinted in *The Argument of the Action*, 2000.

"XRH and DEI in Plato and Others." *Glotta* 43, nos. 3–4 (1965): 285–298.

"Two Notes on Aeschylus' *Septem*." In two parts: *Wiener Studien* NF 1 (1967):

22–30, NF 2 (1968): 5–17. Reprinted in *Sacred Transgressions*: *A Reading of Sophocles' Antigone*. South Bend, Ind.: St. Augustine's Press, 1999.

"Hesiod's *Works and Days*: A First Reading." *Agon* 1 (1967): 150–174.

"The *Aristeia* of Diomedes and the Plot of the *Illiad*." *Agon* 2 (1968): 10–38. Reprinted in *The Argument of the Action*, 2000.

Herodotean Inquiries. The Hague: Martinus Nijhoff, 1969. New edition with "Second Thoughts," South Bend, Ind.: St. Augustine's Press, 1999.

"On Plato's *Timaeus* and Timaeus' Science Fiction." *Interpretation* 2, no. 1 (Summer 1971): 21–63.

Review of H. Lloyd-Jones's translation of Aeschylus' *Oresteia*. *American Journal of Philology* 93, no. 4 (1972): 633–635.

"Aristotle *de anima* III.3–5." *Review of Metaphysics* 28, no. 4 (June 1975): 611–622.

"A Reading of Sophocles' *Antigone*." In three parts: *Interpretation* 4, no. 3 (Spring 1975): 148–196; 5, no. 1 (Summer 1975): 1–55; 5, no. 2 (Winter 1975): 148–184. Reprinted as *Sacred Transgressions*: *A Reading of Sophocles' Antigone*. South Bend, Ind.: St. Augustine's Press, 1999.

"Euripides' *Hippolytus*." In *Essays in Honor of Jacob Klein*, 21–27. Annapolis, Md.: St. John's College Press, 1976. Reprinted in *The Argument of the Action*, 2000.

"The Grammar of Being." *Review of Metaphysics* 30, no. 3 (1977): 486–496.

"Glorifying the Archaic." Review of Hermann Fraenkel, *Early Greek Poetry and Philosophy*. *New York Review of Books*, March 17, 1977.

"On Wisdom and Philosophy: The First Two Chapters of Aristotle's *Metaphysics* A." *Review of Metaphysics* 32, no. 2 (Dec. 1978): 205–215. Reprinted in *The Argument of the Action*, 2000.

"Leo Strauss' *The City and Man*." *Political Science Reviewer* 8 (1978): 1–20.

"On Greek Tragedy." In *The Great Ideas Today*, 102–143. Chicago: Encyclopedia Britannica, Inc., 1980. Reprinted in *The Argument of the Action*, 2000.

"Plato's *Phaedo*." Manuscript. 1980. Published in *The Argument of the Action*, 2000.

"Physics and Tragedy: On Plato's *Cratylus*." *Ancient Philosophy* 1, no. 2 (1981): 172–140. Reprinted in *The Argument of the Action*, 2000.

"*The Furies* of Aeschylus." Manuscript 1982. Published in *The Argument of the Action*, 2000.

Review of Stanley Rosen, *Plato's Sophist: The Drama of Original and Image*. *Graduate Faculty Philosophy Journal* 10, no. 2 (1985): 167–169.

The Being of the Beautiful: *Plato's "Theaetetus," "Sophist," and "Statesman."* Translation and commentary. Chicago: University of Chicago Press, 1984. Paperback in three volumes with a new introduction, 1986.

"On Interpreting Plato's *Charmides*." *Graduate Faculty Philosophy Journal* 11, no. 2 (1986): 9–36. Reprinted in *The Argument of the Action*, 2000.

Symposium. Translation. In *The Dialogues of Plato*, 231–286, New York: Bantam Books, 1986.

Review of M. Giraedeau, *Les notions juridiques et socials chez Herodote*. *Gnomon* 58, no. 5 (1986): 546–57.

"Cicero's *de legibus* I: Its Plan and Intention." *American Journal of Philology* 108, no. 2 (1987): 295–309. A version of this essay is published in the "Epilogue" of *Plato's "Laws": The Discovery of Being*. Chicago: University of Chicago Press, 2000.

"Protagoras' Myth and *Logos*." Manuscript 1988. Published in *The Argument of the Action*, 2000.

Socrates' Second Sailing: On Plato's Republic. Chicago: University of Chicago Press, 1989. Paperback 1992.

The Rhetoric of Morality and Philosophy: *Plato's "Gorgias" and "Phaedrus."* Chicago: University of Chicago Press, 1991.

"The Plan of the *Statesman*." *Metis*: *Revue d'anthropologie du monde grec ancien* 7, nos. 1–2 (1992): 25–47. Reprinted in *The Argument of the Action*, 2000.

"Plato's *Laches*: A Question of Definition." Manuscript 1992. Published in *The Argument of the Action*, 2000.

The Tragedy and Comedy of Life: *Plato's "Philebus."* Translation and commentary. Chicago: University of Chicago Press, 1993.

"On Plato's *Sophist*." *Review of Metaphysics* 46, no. 4 (June 1993): 747–780. Reprinted in *The Argument of the Action*, 2000

"The Poet-Merchant and the Stranger from the Sea." *The Greeks and the Sea* 59–65. New York: Caratzas, 1993.

"Strauss on Plato." University of Chicago lecture, 1993. Published in *The Argument of the Action*, 2000.

"On Plato's *Symposium*." Munich: Carl Friedrich von Siemens Stiftung, 1994. Reprinted in *The Argument of the Action*, 2000.

"On Plato's *Lysis*." Manuscript 1994. Published in *The Argument of the Action*, 2000.

"The First Crisis in First Philosophy." *Graduate Faculty Philosophy Journal* 18, no. 1 (1995): 237–248. Reprinted in *The Argument of the Action*, 2000.

"The Play of Truth." Review of R. B. Rutherford, *The Art of Plato: Ten Essays in Platonic Interpretation. Boston Book Review*, November 10, 1995: 11–12.

The Bow and the Lyre: A Platonic Reading of the Odyssey. Lanham, Md.: Rowman & Littlefield, 1997.

"Plato's *Theaetetus*: On the Way of the Logos." *Review of Metaphysics* 51, no. 1 (September 1997): 25–53. Reprinted in *The Argument of the Action*, 2000.

Review of Michael Tanner, *Nietzsche*. In *The Great Ideas Today*, 454–458. Chicago: Encyclopedia Britannica, Inc., 1997.

"Plato, True and False." *The New Criterion*, February 1998: 70–74.

"'Night and Day . . .': Parmenides." *Metis: Revue d'anthropologie du monde grec ancient*, 13 (1998): 193–225.

"On the *Timaeus*." Lecture at the Hannah Arendt/Reiner Schurmann Memorial Symposium in Political Philosophy: "The Philosophy of Leo Strauss," New School for Social Research, 1999. Published in *The Argument of the Action*, 2000.

"Metamorphosis and Conversion: Apuleius's *Metamorphoses*." In *Literary Imagination, Ancient and Modern: Essays in Honor of David Grene*, edited by Todd Breyfogle, 155–176. Chicago: University of Chicago Press, 1999.

"On Heraclitus." *Review of Metaphysics* 53, no. 3 (March, 2000): 613–633.

The Argument of the Action: *Essays on Greek Poetry and Philosophy*, edited by Ronna Burger and Michael Davis. Chicago: University of Chicago Press, 2000

Plato's "Laws": *The Discovery of Being*. Chicago: University of Chicago Press, 2000.

"Socrates and Plato: The Dialectics of Eros." German translation in *Über die Liebe*, edited by Heinrich Meier and Gerhardt Neumann. Munich: Piper Verlag, 2000. *Socrates and Plato. The Dialectics of Eros* (German and English). Munich: Carl Friedrich von Siemens Stiftung, 2002.

"Derrida and Plato." Lecture delivered at New York University, in series, "Derrida and his Non-Contemporaries," October 19, 2000.

Plato. *Symposium*. A translation by Seth Benardete, with commentaries by Allan Bloom and Seth Benardete. Chicago: University of Chicago Press, 2001.

"A. E. Housman." [www.greekworks.com] December 15, 2001.

"Plato's *Parmenides*: A Sketch." Manuscript 2001.

Encounters and Reflections: Conversations with Seth Benardete, edited by Ronna Burger. Chicago: University of Chicago Press, 2002.

Aristotle. *On Poetics*. Translation by Seth Benardete and Michael Davis, Introduction by Michael Davis. South Bend, Ind.: St. Augustine Press, 2002.

"The Plan of Odysseus and the Plot of the *Philoctetes*." *Epoche* 7, no. 2 (Spring 2003): 133–150.

"Freedom: Grace and Necessity." *Freedom and the Human Person*, edited by Richard Velkley, *Studies in Philosophy and the History of Philosophy*. Washington, D.C.: The Catholic University of America Press, forthcoming.